William Sidney Tangier Smith

The Geology of Santa Catalina Island

William Sidney Tangier Smith

The Geology of Santa Catalina Island

ISBN/EAN: 9783743319943

Manufactured in Europe, USA, Canada, Australia, Japa

Cover: Foto ©ninafisch / pixelio.de

Manufactured and distributed by brebook publishing software (www.brebook.com)

William Sidney Tangier Smith

The Geology of Santa Catalina Island

THE GEOLOGY OF SANTA CATALINA ISLAND.

BY WILLIAM SIDNEY TANGIER SMITH.
Candidate Ph. D., University of California.

CONTENTS.

PLATES I—III.

		PAGE.
I.	INTRODUCTION	2
	1. LITERATURE	2
	2. GENERAL DESCRIPTION	3
II.	TOPOGRAPHY	5
	1. MAJOR FEATURES	4
	Main Ridge	4
	Types of Topography	5
	Slope of Summits	6
	Two Types of Drainage	7
	2. MINOR FEATURES	8
	Echo Lake	8
	Sea Cliffs	9
	Bays	10
	Beaches	10
	Terraces	11
III.	GEOLOGY	13
	A. ERUPTIVE ROCKS	14
	1. DIORITE	14
	Macroscopic Characters	14
	Microscopic Characters	15
	2. PORPHYRITE	19
	Occurrence	19
	Character	19
	Macroscopic Characters	20
	Microscopic Characters	20
	Analysis	25
	Inliers of Basement Rocks	25
	Porphyrite Dykes	26
	3. RHYOLITE	28
	Occurrence	28
	Macroscopic Characters	28
	Microscopic Characters	29
	4. ANDESITE	30
	Occurrence	30
	Macroscopic Characters	31
	Microscopic Characters	32
	Glassy Facies	35
	Basaltic Facies	37
	Analysis	41

January 12, 1897.

			PAGE.
	5.	Relative Age	41
B.	Tuff and Diatomaceous Earth		42
	1.	Occurrence	42
	2.	Tuff	43
	3.	Shale	43
		Microscopic Characters	44
		Character of the Organic Remains	45
		Chemical Characters	48
		Origin of the Shale	49
		Analysis of Limestone	50
C.	Sedimentary Deposits		51
D.	Breccia		52
E.	Basement Series		54
	1.	Quartzite	54
		Macroscopic Characters	55
		Microscopic Characters	57
	2.	Actinolite and Hornblende Schists	58
	3.	Serpentine	58
	4.	Talc-Schist	60
	5.	Origin of the Serpentines	61
	6.	Garnet-Amphibolite	62
IV.	Geomorphogeny		65
	1.	Submarine Topography	65
	2.	Outline of History	67

I. Introduction.

1. Literature.

The existing literature bearing upon the geology of Santa Catalina is very limited, consisting of a short note in Whitney's Geology,[1] a brief report[2] and other scattered notes in the various Annual Reports of the State Mining Bureau, and a recent account of the topography of the island, by Prof. Lawson.[3] The report of the State Mining Bureau is not only superficial, but very inaccurate. In Whitney's report the absence of terraces is noted, contrasting with the neighboring islands, and the suggestion is made that this island may be sinking. Both of these points are elaborated

---

[1] Geol. Surv. of Cal., Geol., Vol. I, pp. 182-186.
[2] Tenth An. Rept., State Mineralogist, pp. 277-281.
[3] "The Post-Pliocene Diastrophism of the Coast of Southern California," by Andrew C. Lawson. Bull. Dept. Geol., Univ. Cal., Vol. I, No. 4, pp. 135-139.

by Prof. Lawson, who further calls attention to the older topography of this island.

2. GENERAL DESCRIPTION.

Santa Catalina Island, one of the group known as the Channel Islands, off the coast of southern California, lies about 20 miles south of San Pedro Hill, the nearest point on the mainland. At about the same distance south of Santa Catalina lies the island of San Clemente, the three elevations being nearly in a straight line.

The general trend of the island is northwest by west. Its length is approximately twenty-one miles, with an average width of three miles, varying from half a mile at the isthmus to about eight miles in the widest part. The prevailing winds are from west to southwest, and the waves exert their greatest force on the southwest face of the island. They are, however, by no means inactive on the landward side, as is shown by the rapidly retreating shore-line.

The only settlements on the island are the summer resort at Avalon, and a small community at the isthmus. Besides these, a few solitary houses are located at different points on the coast. The island was once occupied by Indians, and evidences of their camps occur frequently in the form of shell fragments, rounded stone implements, and earth blackened by the camp fires. Owing to its ruggedness and the scarcity of water, the island is habitable in only a few places. There are half a dozen or more springs and creeks which do not dry up during the summer, and a few wells supply the other points. All the water is decidedly alkaline.

The vegetation consists chiefly of herbage and shrubbery or underbrush, cactus forming an important part. The larger trees, except for a few dwarf oaks, are confined to the bottoms of the cañons. The summits, in general, are bare of everything except grass and cactus, but the majority of the slopes are thickly covered with an often impenetrable growth of scrub-oak, greasewood *(Adenostoma fasciculatum?)*, and elder, intermingled with cactus. It is noteworthy that, in spite of the oftentimes luxuriant vegetation, the soil-covering is generally very thin, and the underlying formations are constantly exposed.

II. Topography.

1. Major Features.

Main Ridge.—The island is traversed from end to end by a single main ridge, with branch ridges running out on either

Figure 1—The Isthmus, looking south.

side. Beginning about a mile from the southeastern extremity of the island, this ridge makes a bold sweep around the head of Avalon Cañon to a point nearly west of Avalon. There it makes an abrupt turn, almost at right angles, and then follows very nearly the line of the northern coast, at an average distance of about a mile from the shore, till it reaches the isthmus. (See fig. 1.) This is a low divide, in the form of a saddle, with very gentle slopes. It has a length, between the bounding hills, of less than a quarter of a mile, and its greatest elevation is about twenty feet. At either end of the isthmus the hills rise very abruptly to the main ridge, which is here from 800 to 900 feet in height. West of this point the ridge has two divisions, which unite, less than a mile and a half beyond, to form again a single ridge, continuing to the end of the island. On this end the ridge lies nearer the south than the north shore. One noticeable feature of this main watershed is the general uniformity of its height. For the greater part of its length the variations in altitude are not more than two or three hundred feet, the average elevation being about 1,400 feet. The two greatest elevations are near the center of the island, the peak known as "Orizaba" (or "Brush Mountain"), marked 2,109 feet on the map, and "Black Jack," the peak about a mile to the northeast of this, about a hundred feet lower.

Types of Topography.—The general character of the topography is very bold and rugged, and shows an advanced stage of development. A general view of the island from almost any point gives an impression of a close succession of sharp, steep ridges and V-shaped cañons. One of the most marked examples of this effect is in the slopes of Avalon Cañon, particularly on the west side, when seen from the opposite summits.

Viewed in detail, the island shows two prevailing forms of topographic relief: (1) the sharp ridges and V-shaped cañons just referred to, and (2) the rounded and level forms belonging to an older topography. The slope of the cañon walls, in the first type, is usually steep, occasionally having an angle of 40° or over. The first form is the prevailing one in most parts of the island, masking the remnants of the second.

The second type of topography is strongly contrasted with the first. It is found in the higher parts of the island, best developed in the eastern end. It is shown in the level character of the main ridge, and of several of the minor ridges which approximate it in altitude. These latter are (1) the principal ridges between Middle Ranch Cañon and the main ridge bounding Avalon Cañon on the west; (2) the ridge connecting the main ridge with the point north of Whitley's Cove; and (3) a portion of each of the ridges running from the main ridge into the Little Harbor region (which comprises the semicircular area within a general radius of about three miles from Little Harbor).

In the lower portions of the Little Harbor region this second type of topography again appears. Within this area the tributary ridges, radiating from a central point not far from Little Harbor, rise to the higher slopes by a long, moderate incline. Beginning at the shore-line, with a cliff of from 200 to 300 feet, the rise above this is very gradual, till, at an average distance of a mile and a half from the water, a height of about 600 or 700 feet is reached. Beyond this the grade increases, and an altitude equal to that of the main ridge is soon reached, usually some little distance from the main ridge itself. Standing on the lower and more level portion of this area, and looking either toward the isthmus or in the opposite direction, one sees a great amphitheater, the distant ridges rising one above another, like gigantic tiers of seats, up to the main ridge. Were it not for the recent stream erosion we should thus have in the immediate neighborhood of Little Harbor an almost even surface, with a gentle seaward slope. The present drainage, however, has dissected this surface, cutting channels some of which, in their lower stretches, have a width of 100 yards or more, and a depth of perhaps 200 feet. In places the streams have made considerable deposits, and at a number of points these have been cut through, in very recent times, to a maximum depth of about twenty-five feet, at some distance from the shore.

Slope of Summits.—It has been seen that the main ridge and certain of the branch ridges are, in a general way, level in the direction of the length of the island. In those portions of the main ridge on either side of Avalon Cañon which are oblique to the trend of the island, the generally level summits are seen to slope at an angle of a little over one degree toward the northern shore. (See figs. 2 and 3.) In fig. 2, Black Jack and Orizaba and a portion of the ridge between Silver and Middle Ranch Cañons are seen above the main ridge. At the " west end " (that por-

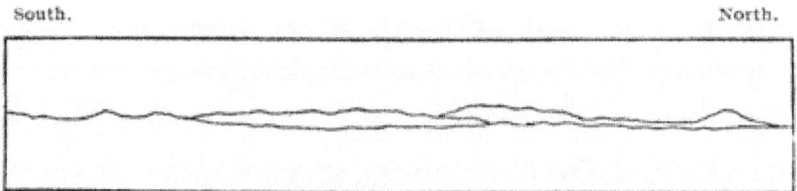

FIGURE 2—Outline of the summit of the main ridge west of Avalon Cañon, as seen from the summit of the ridge on the opposite side of the cañon.

tion of the island west of the isthmus), the more northerly of the two branches of the main ridge has an average height throughout its length, about 200 feet lower than the other. Thus it appears that in transverse section the island shows a general slope toward the mainland.

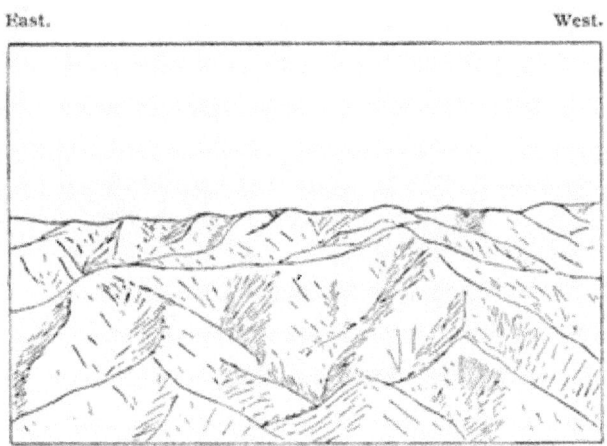

FIGURE 3—Outline of the summit of the main ridge south of Avalon Cañon, as seen from the summit of the ridge on the opposite side of the cañon.

Two Types of Drainage.—The principal stream cañons running from the main watershed are of two types, which may be readily distinguished on the map. Those cañons which have their mouths on the northern or landward coast are broad and open stream valleys, while those running down to the opposite shore have a long and trough-like character which they preserve to the shore-line. These two types are quite pronounced over all the southeastern division of the island, while at the isthmus the two harbors — which are merely submerged stream valleys — still show the same contrast. In the western end this characteristic, though still evident, is not so marked. The narrow, trough-like cañons are occasionally somewhat broader in their upper portions than near their mouths, where they are frequently mere rocky gorges. The most pronounced example of the narrow type is Silver Cañon, whose walls near the mouth rise to a height of over 1,000 feet, while the distance between them at the base is in places not more than from twenty-five to a hundred feet. The length of this cañon is about three miles. Avalon Cañon, a good example of the other type, has a length of about two miles, with a mean width, from watershed to watershed, of somewhat more than that. From the main ridge on either side a great number of rather short and steep V-shaped cañons are tributary to the main valley, these stream beds making the descent of 1,200 or 1,400 feet within an average distance of about a mile.

All the forms of topography thus far described are largely independent of the material from which they are carved; that is, variation in the character of the rocks has but little connection with variation in topographic form.

2. Minor Features.

Echo Lake.—There is one small lake on the island, situated about a mile to the northeast of Black Jack, at an altitude of about 1,300 feet. This belongs to the class of ephemeral lakes. Visiting it two summers in succession, at the same season, the writer found it, the first time, a shallow pond about 100 yards long, while the next year it was entirely dry. It is a small drainage lake, without outlet, probably shut in by faulting.

Sea Cliffs.—Except for the openings formed by the cañon mouths, cliffs surround the island on all sides, running from one or two hundred feet to 1,400 feet or more in height. The boldest and highest cliffs are found at the west end, and between Silver Cañon and the southeastern extremity of the island. The highest of all are just to the east of Silver Cañon, where the waves have cut across the end of a minor ridge whose altitude equals that of the main ridge. These cliffs, although furnishing excellent geological sections, are wholly inaccessible at nearly all points, owing to their height, the angle at which they meet the water, and the absence of beaches.

The cliffs are rapidly receding, in many cases more rapidly than the streams which trench their surfaces can cut down their channels. This is shown by the V-shaped openings on the face of the cliff, from 50 to 200 feet or more above the water. Such are the mouths of the cañons draining the southern slopes of the main ridge at the head of Avalon Cañon. These open on the southern coast, about two miles to the east of the entrance to Silver Cañon. The rapidity of the cliff-cutting here will appear the more remarkable when it is known that these streams, though draining comparatively small areas, are torrential in character. It must, however, be remembered that they are active only during the rainy season.[1]

In addition to these larger V-shaped openings, several smaller ones were seen along the higher parts of the cliff, less than a mile to the east of the entrance to Silver Cañon. These, from the water side, present the appearance of a stream draining outward over the face of the cliff. From above, however, it is seen that the drainage is inland, toward Silver Cañon. This phenomenon is due to the cutting back

---

[1] A phenomenon similar to that above described has been observed by the writer at several points along the California coast between Port Harford and Santa Monica. Here the recent streams have carved narrow channels in the surface of the lowest terraces which border the shore, and have formed clear-cut V's on their upper edge. The cause here (unlike that in the case of Santa Catalina) is, no doubt, that an insufficient time has elapsed, since the elevation of the coast, for the streams to deepen their channels further.

of the watershed so rapidly that the drainage has not had time to adjust itself to the changed conditions.

Bays.—The coast of the island, particularly on the landward side, is indented with numerous bays. On the north side, partly on account of less active cutting along the coast, and partly on account of the more open cañons whose submergence has produced the bays, they are wider, and generally furnish safe landing places. On the other side of the island, although there are numerous recesses in the shore-line (particularly of the west end), these openings are generally surrounded by high cliffs, and there are only two bays, Catalina Harbor at the isthmus, and Little Harbor.

Beaches.—Several cañons on the south side of the island, while not forming bays, have beaches at their mouths. In many cases, both here and on the northern coast, the beaches have been built up by wave action so as to form along the shore a barrier from five to ten feet higher than the area just behind. The beaches, in general, consist of coarse, well rounded, and flattened shingle, though one or two exceptions were seen where the beach was largely composed of a rather fine sand. Apart from the beaches which mark the entrance to the larger cañons, there are a few very narrow beaches for short stretches at the base of the cliffs, only on the landward side. These are in general accessible only at low water.

The beaches as a rule are curved in outline, concave toward the ocean. A marked exception to this is seen in the projecting, tongue-like, Pebbly Beach. This has been built up by the opposing action of two series of waves, which, coming from either direction along the coast, meet at this point. Not only does the beach exhibit the barrier-like character mentioned above, but its outer surface shows a series of narrow terraces formed by the waves. As many as six were seen at one point.

Another form is shown in the hook which marks the entrance to Catalina Harbor, and is known as Ballast Point. This is built of coarse shingle, some of the material composing it having a diameter of about a foot. High winds blow daily through the narrow pass at the isthmus, causing a strong inward current, which is gradually bringing about a shoaling of the harbor. Thus here, as at Pebbly Beach, the accumulation of shore-drift, through the action of waves and currents, has more than kept pace with the sinking of the island.

Terraces.—The pronounced contrast which Santa Catalina presents in its topography, not only to the adjacent land areas, but to the greater part of the coast of California, has already been shown by Prof. Lawson.[1] The most striking difference is in the marked absence, on this island, of the terraces which are so clear-cut and pronounced on the slopes of San Pedro Hill and San Clemente. With but two exceptions, Santa Catalina is devoid of any evident terracing from one end to the other. The terrace-like character of the lower levels of the Little Harbor region (already described) forms one of these exceptions. That this is, in part, at least, of the nature of a true terrace, is shown by the nearly level character of the various ridges in their lower parts, their gentle seaward slope, the change in grade at the rear, at an altitude of 600 or 700 feet, the planing off of the upturned beds of the basement series, with rolled pebbles scattered over the lower slopes of the andesite, besides more or less sandstone and conglomerate on these slopes bordering Middle Ranch Cañon. All these point to a time when this region contained a bay, into an arm of which a stream, doubtless an older form of that which now drains Middle Ranch Cañon, brought the deposits just mentioned (shown on the map). It is possible that there is, besides this, a series of such terraces within this area. If so they are not strongly marked, and the fact could only be established by a more detailed observation than the writer had time for. Terracing similar to that found here must at one time have ex-

---

[1] "The Post-Pliocene Diastrophism of the Coast of Southern California," by Andrew C. Lawson. Bull. Dept. Geol., Univ. Cal., Vol. I, No. 4, pp. 135-139.

tended along the cliffs bordering the island,[1] but it has been since removed by a prolonged period of active cliff erosion. That the evidence is preserved here is due to the fact that the terracing extended so far inland. This belongs to an earlier period than the terraces of the main coast and of San Clemente.

The other terraced structure occurs in the cañon back of

FIGURE 4—Dissected alluvial fan, southeast side of Avalon Cañon.

Avalon (see fig. 4), about half a mile from the shore-line, and is seen on both sides of the cañon—which is about a quarter of a mile wide at this point—as a broad platform extending up some distance into the cañon-like opening on either side of the main valley. Its front edge has a gentle seaward slope, while from front to rear it rises gradually toward the hills. A sharp ascent of about forty or fifty feet marks the

---

[1] Rolled pebbles were found scattered over a small area near the southeastern end of the island, at an altitude of 1,000 feet; also on the main ridge south of Avalon Cañon, at about 1,400 feet; but the remains of an Indian camp within a hundred feet, in each case, made the evidence doubtful. In neither case, however, were any pebbles found among the remains marking the camp.

front of the platforms on either side of the cañon. Streams have cut into the surface and along the sides, forming several comparatively broad watercourses. Some of these streams have not yet reached the level of the main cañon where they debouch upon it, and have formed small, rather low and broad alluvial fans beyond their mouths.

The material composing the platforms consists of both rounded and angular fragments. From the form of the structures and the form and arrangement of their material, it is evident that we have here, not a stream terrace, as its appearance might at first indicate, but undoubted alluvial fans.[1] These have been dissected and cut away in recent geological times, owing to the drowning of the stream valley at Avalon, with a consequent shortening of the stream courses, and a deepening of the channels.

III. Geology.

The basement series of Santa Catalina consists of crystalline metamorphic rocks, principally quartzite. This series, with the hornblendic rocks, the talc-schist and the serpentine, covers in a general way the whole western half of the island. Besides the main occurrence, there are patches of these rocks along the main ridge to the west of Avalon Cañon. The basement rocks are cut by occasional dikes, which are principally at the west end, and have a general northeasterly trend.

The eastern end of the island is occupied by diorite and porphyrite. Bordering this area on the north, and of later age, is an area consisting of numerous flows of andesite, of which there are several other smaller occurrences besides. A particularly interesting area of these rocks is found to the east of Isthmus Cove, where, interbedded with the volcanics, is seen a band of tuff and diatomaceous earth.

The lower slopes of the andesites in the Little Harbor

---

[1] Alluvial fans are by no means uncommon on the island, but no other case presents any similar terracing.

region are covered with rolled pebbles, with several patches of sedimentary deposits. In the eastern portion of the Little Harbor region is a small area of rhyolite, which was not found elsewhere. A narrow strip of quartzite breccia occurs at the southeastern extremity of the island.

A. ERUPTIVE ROCKS.

1. DIORITE.

There are three observed occurrences of the diorite: one along the cliff bordering the shore just to the north of Avalon, the second near the head of the cañon back of Pebbly Beach, and the third in the lower portion of Silver Cañon. These are apparently dikes of considerable width.

Macroscopic Characters.—The diorite is coarse-grained, and of a light grayish color, more or less mottled. The specific gravity of a specimen from Silver Cañon was found to be 2.777. In the coarser-grained specimens the separate minerals may easily be seen without recourse to a lens. With the lens the rock is seen to be composed of a ferromagnesian mineral, feldspar and a varying amount of quartz.

The feldspars range from a somewhat glassy condition to one in which they are whitish and more or less opaque. They constitute, in general, the principal mineral of the diorite. The ferromagnesian mineral is hornblende, dark green in color, and altered in part to chlorite. This mineral varies in amount from a little less than one-half to perhaps one-fifth of the surface area. Besides the hornblende an occasional leaflet of biotite was seen in the specimens from near Avalon, and also in one or two from Silver Cañon. The quartz usually occurs in small areas scattered throughout the mass of the rock. In addition to these, magnetite is apparent in nearly all the hand-specimens of the coarser-grained varieties, being rather conspicuous in one specimen from the cañon back of Pebbly Beach.

Microscopic Characters.—Under the microscope the diorites are found to have a nearly even-grained, holocrystalline structure, and to be composed essentially of a lime-soda-feldspar, hornblende and occasional biotite, with free quartz always present in varying amounts. Augite is also present in some of the slides, and in nearly all magnetite is an important constituent. No apatite was observed in any of the sections. There is an occasional tendency to a porphyritic development among the feldspars. Mineralogically considered, the rock is a quartz-hornblende-diorite, with a tendency to lath-shaped forms among the feldspars.

The feldspars are in general allotriomorphic, and tend to develop crystal faces only occasionally, where they come in contact with quartz. In some of the slides many of the feldspars are fairly clear and free from inclusions or decomposition products. Aside from these the majority are clouded by alteration products, which, in some cases, have partly or wholly obliterated the traces of the twinning lamellæ, which are clearly shown in the fresher material. This cloudiness is apparently due in part to a kaolinization of the plagioclase, but also to calcite, which occurs in small, irregular patches and threads in many of the sections. This product is also found, in some instances, in lines along the twinning planes. Twinning takes place according to the Carlsbad, albite and pericline laws. Pericline twinning is the least frequent, and is usually seen under crossed nicols as a series of very fine lines.

Excellent zonal structure is occasionally seen, but is infrequent. The varying optical orientation in such cases shows that the mineral grows more acid from the center outward. Inclusions in the feldspars are not common, but rarely one of the largest crystals contains from one to a number of smaller feldspars which are without definite orientation toward their host, and without good crystal boundaries. Inclusions of small ragged flakes of hornblende or chloritic material are of much more frequent occurrence. Several feldspars occur packed with small, irregularly bounded sections of what appears to be primary hornblende.

The structure in this case is micropoikilitic. Occasionally sections contain numerous brightly polarizing, microscopic needles, doubtless of hornblende.

Besides the decomposition products already mentioned, more or less epidote is usually present, generally in small irregular patches.

All the diorites have doubtless been subject to stresses since they were consolidated, but only the rocks from Silver Cañon give any marked microscopic evidence of it. In these rocks the feldspars seem to have been particularly affected, the hornblende and quartz showing little or no evidence of strain. The evidence here is of three kinds—altered optical properties, bent crystals and fractures, which may or may not cause displacements. The extinction of the feldspars is frequently very indefinite and variable. Comparatively few of them show good extinction, and even these are sometimes considerably affected by cracks. In the others strain shadows take the place of the normal extinction. Bent crystals are not common, but a few of the sections show a distinct curvature, and a corresponding alteration in extinction. The fractures referred to are not the cracks frequently found in single individuals, but more extensive ones passing from crystal to crystal, simply as cracks, or forming veins which have been filled with secondary matter. A few veins were found, the most pronounced one extending irregularly half through a slide, some of the feldspars on either side having suffered slight displacement. This vein is .05 mm. in width, and is filled principally with calcite, with more or less chlorite and quartz.

From the extinction angles on either side of the albite lamellæ, in favorable sections, the plagioclase appears to lie between a basic oligoclase and an acid labradorite.

From its relations to the quartz and feldspars, the hornblende seems to have been the first mineral in the order of the crystallization of the essential constituents of the diorite. The relations of quartz and feldspar show that a part of the feldspar was formed before, and part at the same time with the quartz. The simultaneous development with the quartz is evidenced by a frequent irregular intergrowth along the boundary line of the two minerals, and further by the occasional development of micropegmatitic structure.

Quartz occurs in somewhat smaller individuals than do the feldspars. It is most frequently found in aggregations or in lines, as if, being the last mineral to form, it had filled the spaces between those previously existing. It is present in varying amount in all the slides, being fairly abundant in some, amounting to perhaps one-fourth of the total minerals of the slide. The sections vary in size from about .1 mm. to about 1.2 mm. It occurs in allotriomorphic forms, usually with very irregular outlines, the sections being frequently somewhat intergrown on the margins. The sections are usually clear. Most of them contain liquid inclusions, occurring usually without any definite arrangement, though occasionally they are seen in lines extending through several sections. Besides these there may be seen with the higher powers occasional minute, greenish needles, and sections having the form of cross-sections of hornblende. They are without noticeable polarization. The quartz also contains occasional magnetite.

The hornblende occurs in sections with very irregular boundaries, due to resorption. No approach to crystal forms was seen. The feldspar is always moulded on the hornblende, except in one case observed. In this section a small crystal of feldspar was seen apparently projecting into one side of the hornblende, the feldspar showing good crystal boundaries where surrounded by the hornblende. Aside from this instance the hornblendes contain no inclusions of feldspar, while the feldspars contain occasional inclusions of hornblendic material. The smaller feldspars are doubtless, in part, at least, contemporaneous with the hornblendes, though the feldspars in general are later. In size the former compare favorably with the feldspars. Twinning parallel to the orthopinacoid is common in the larger and fresher sections. The pleochroism is pronounced,

c being green, b yellowish brown, and a pale yellow-green to almost colorless. The absorption formula is $c > b > a$. Inclusions are not common and are principally magnetite. There is an occasional intergrowth with biotite. The alteration of the hornblende is well advanced in many of the slides. It appears to be undergoing a uralitic change by which it is transformed into a dirty greenish, fibrous aggregate, much like "reedy hornblende," with a rather weak pleochroism. This secondary hornblende has usually a parallel arrangement of its fibres, and the terminals of the sections are generally more or less ragged. It also occurs in finely fibrous, irregular areas, with the fibres irregularly oriented. A further alteration of the hornblende is mainly into chlorite and calcite.

Biotite is not common, though occasionally found. The sections are strongly pleochroic, always show irregular boundaries, and the mineral occurs either alone or intergrown with hornblende. The biotite is in part altered to chlorite, and some of its sections are wholly surrounded by a chloritic margin. No inclusions occur, except occasional grains of magnetite.

Augite is present in some of the slides, being variable in amount, but at times forming an important constituent. It generally presents very irregular boundaries, but several sections were seen showing roughly the crystal form characteristic of cross-sections of augite. It has a granular, much broken appearance, and a high refractive index. Its most characteristic feature is a clouding of the area by an opaque, dirty-brown decomposition product. Few of the sections were free from this product, and it marked the mineral wherever found. The augite is practically colorless, and is without any sensible pleochroism. No cleavage was observed anywhere, and only one case of twinning. Whereever the augite comes in contact with the hornblende the boundary line is sharp and clear. When it occurs in isolated sections these are usually free from the uralitic product described in connection with the hornblende. This, together with the freedom of all the hornblende areas from the cloudy decomposition product of the augite, naturally leads to the conclusion that none of the fibrous hornblende comes from the augite.

Magnetite is found in all the slides, though not in any considerable amount. It occurs as inclusions in the other minerals, and is generally in the form of grains frequently showing partial crystal boundaries. In size they range up to .3 mm. Besides the grains, there are several very irregular areas of considerable size—up to 2 mm. or more in length—in or near the areas of the ferromagnesian minerals.

2. PORPHYRITE.

Following the usage of Iddings[1] the term "porphyrite" is here used to include those rocks which are characterized by a medium-grained porphyritic structure, and which contain among their essential constituents a lime-soda-feldspar. They constitute the connecting link, as it were, between the deep-seated diorites on the one hand, and the surficial andesitic rocks on the other, and pass by insensible gradations into either. The physical conditions attending and controlling its crystallization are the prime factor in determining the position of the rock in the scheme of classification.

Occurrence.—The porphyrite occurs in a single large area in the southeastern part of the island, and was not found elsewhere by the writer, except as smaller masses in the form of dikes. The main area has an average width of about three miles, with an extreme length of about nine. It is cut by dikes of porphyrite and diorite, from two to thirty feet or more in width, which are shown on the cliffs at a number of places along the shore.

Character.—The rocks are very much weathered, and even those specimens which appeared to be fairly fresh were seen, when examined microscopically, to be considerably altered. In weathering the rocks first break into coarse,

---

[1] Twelfth An. Rept. U. S. Geol. Surv., Part I, pp. 582-584.

irregular, block-like forms, looking, in some cases along the shore near Avalon, like square pillars projecting from the side of the cliff. These break up into smaller block-like masses, and the process is continued until the gravelly condition is reached. On the hill slopes the projecting masses frequently present similar forms with smooth surfaces, but it is not uncommon to see also small, boss-like projections, with rough, uneven surfaces. The cause of this difference in form is doubtless a variation in the grain of the rock. The soil formed from these rocks is generally of a dull, yellowish color. The porphyrite contains the same minerals that occur in the diorite, except biotite, which was not seen in any of the slides. It presents the same general characters wherever found.

Macroscopic Characters.—The color of both the unaltered and weathered porphyrite is much the same as that of the diorite, the fresh hand-specimens varying from light to dark gray, most of them with a tinge of green. Little can be made out in the fresher specimens with the unaided eye, except an occasional feldspar, shown by the reflection from a cleavage surface. Hornblende crystals of some length—up to 5 mm. or more—are developed in one or two specimens. As the rock weathers the whitening of the feldspars usually brings out plainly the porphyritic structure. With the lens the porphyritic feldspars may occasionally be distinguished from the medium-grained ground-mass, though these are usually masked more or less by the fracture of the rock, which leaves minute flakes or splinters clinging to the surface of the specimen. The rock frequently presents a slightly mottled surface, in the dark and light colors. Gleaming bits of pyrite may occasionally be seen in some of the specimens.

Microscopic Characters.—Microscopically the rock is holocrystalline and porphyritic, with phenocrysts of a lime-soda-feldspar and of hornblende—occasionally also of augite—and a medium-grained granular ground-mass, composed essentially of feldspar and quartz. The phenocrysts vary considerably in number. In some slides there are comparatively few, while in others they constitute the larger portion of the slide. The ground-mass is never glassy, and does not show any flow structure, except to a slight extent in specimens from one or two dikes. Quartz is seen sometimes among the phenocrysts, though this is a very rare occurrence. Magnetite occurs as an accessory, but usually in very small amounts. No apatite was seen, and in the rock of which the analysis is given below no phosphorus was found. Most sections show little evidence of disturbance.

The porphyritic feldspars occur in idiomorphic forms, which are somewhat tabular parallel to the brachypinacoid. The majority of the crystals show good boundaries, except where their growth was interfered with by the growth of other phenocrysts. Many of the sections, however, show boundaries which are more or less irregular or rounded, and due, in part, at least, to resorption. The sections vary in size from about .2 mm. to nearly 3 mm. Zoning is common. The twinning is in accordance with the albite and Carlsbad laws. Pericline twinning rarely occurs. As in the diorite, the feldspar lies between a basic oligoclase and an acid labradorite. Many of the sections are considerably cracked. Some of the feldspars are fairly fresh, but most of them are more or less clouded by decomposition products. This cloudiness is due largely to a kaolinization of the mineral. Considerable areas are sometimes altered to calcite, with more or less epidote. The decomposition is such at times as to destroy, partly or wholly, the traces of twinning. Occasional inclusions of hornblende or chlorite are seen in the feldspars. One section was seen with a zone of chloritic material not far from the boundary, arranged in threads and fibres parallel to the longer direction of the feldspar. Small magnetite grains are rarely included in the feldspar.

The hornblende is prismatic in habit, and usually either shows resorbed boundaries, or the original outlines are more or less obliterated by alteration products. No terminal planes were seen in any section. In two or three of the slides the characteristic lozenge-shaped cross-sections were seen, with a distinct prismatic cleavage. Twinning is common, parallel to the orthopinacoid. Comparatively few unaltered sections were found, most of the hornblende which was originally present in the slides having been altered to chlorite and calcite. In some of the slides the hornblende is wholly replaced by secondary minerals. The freshest sections are frequently surrounded by a chloritic border, or decomposition has begun along cracks and cleavage planes. The pleochroism of both chlorite and hornblende is the same as in the diorites. The hornblende in some cases has the fibrous character described under the diorites. In one slide in which this fibrous hornblende occurs, without good crystal boundaries, there is another secondary hornblende, with different optical properties, and having the form characteristic of augite.

From what has been said it will be seen that hornblende is a primary constituent of the rock. It is also the dominant ferromagnesian mineral. Roughly estimated, it constitutes, with its decomposition products, about one-fourth or one-third of the total amount of minerals in the slides.

Augite is found in varying amounts in nearly all the slides, usually in the form of irregular grains, or as irregular brownish or more or less opaque patches. It has the same general structure and habit as in the diorite and its decomposition products are similar. Usually it has a very insignificant position compared with the other minerals of the rock. In two or three of the slides, however, it compares in amount with the hornblende, and in one slide in particular—from a specimen from the cañon back of Avalon—the sections, though rather small, are quite numerous, constituting perhaps one-fifth or one-fourth of the total minerals of the slide. Here the mineral is fairly fresh and free from decomposition products.

It is almost colorless or pale green, and without pleochroism. When any crystal boundaries are shown they are only partial. The form when developed shows the usual octagonal cross-section. The crystals occur as separate individuals. The feldspars are molded on the augites, and sometimes completely enclose the smaller sections. The augite shows no definite cleavage, but is usually more or less traversed by cracks. In this slide no hornblende was seen, though there are considerable areas of chlorite. No doubt hornblende was at one time present, being now represented by the chlorite, for the augite in the slide has no border of chlorite, nor is the latter seen along the cracks of that mineral. When near or touching chloritic areas the augites have as sharp boundaries and appear quite as fresh as those sections which have no chlorite near them. In weathering the augite alters to a granular, dirty brownish product, more or less opaque. In one slide, from the northern side of Avalon cañon, what was originally augite with a short prismatic habit, is entirely altered to hornblende (see page 22). The sections are idiomorphic, with the forms characteristic of augite, but with the cleavage of hornblende. In vertical sections the cleavage is very pronounced, showing in part as open cracks. This hornblende is pleochroic, a being a very pale yellow, b pale yellowish green, c greenish brown. The mineral is more or less dull in appearance, and the polarization colors are not clear. It is quite unlike the fibrous hornblende in character. One of the sections shows indistinct twinning lamellæ parallel to the orthopinacoid. The augites contain as inclusions occasional magnetite grains.

The magnetite varies greatly in amount, being almost entirely absent from some of the sections. In the rock containing abundant augite there is considerable magnetite in small, irregular patches or needle-like forms, at times in or cutting across the feldspars, or projecting into the augites. One slide from Pebbly Beach shows a few small grains with the crystal form of magnetite, but altered to limonite.

The granular ground-mass of the porphyrite is composed of usually allotriomorphic feldspar and quartz, the larger proportion being of the former. At times, however, the feldspars tend to lath-shaped or rectangular forms. The borders of the grains in the ground-mass frequently interlock. Occasionally small, ragged flakes of hornblende or small patches of chlorite occur. The minerals of the ground-mass, in those slides showing the most pronounced porphyritic structure, have a diameter of from .03 mm. to .1 mm. As the size of the grains increases the rock assumes the structure of diorite-porphyrite, with occasional, though rare, porphyritic quartzes. All gradations were found between porphyrite and diorite.

The quartz varies considerably in amount in the porphyritic rocks. Usually it is rather subordinate, but occasionally it is quite abundant, forming perhaps one-fourth of the minerals of the slide. These rocks, however, are not common, and are doubtless only local developments. One slide of the diorite-porphyrite is remarkable for the manner in which the quartz is developed with respect to the other minerals. This rock (from the slopes to the west of the entrance to Silver Cañon) contains abundant phenocrysts of feldspar, with porphyritically developed quartz. Under crossed nicols the quartz appears as scattered and more or less rounded grains. Occasionally several of these are found near together, showing similar polarization colors and a common extinction. On revolving the stage it is seen that the rounded borders do not mark the limit of the sections of quartz; for the extinction of the mineral shows that it has an outer zone which has a pronounced micropoikilitic structure, being closely packed with finely polarizing feldspars. The quartz occasionally shows a crystal form. The ground-mass of the rock is coarsely crystalline and consists largely of micropoikilitic quartz similar to the larger sections, but without clear centers. A very few of the larger sections also are wholly filled with feldspar aggregates. The clear centers together with the micropoikilitic margins indicate arrested development of the quartz, which began to form before the growth of the minute feldspars, the latter forming before the final crystallization of the quartz. The rock is much altered, and except in one or two instances the traces of twinning in the feldspar phenocrysts are wholly obliterated by decomposition products. Hornblende is wholly replaced by chloritic material.

Analysis.—The porphyrite was nowhere found in an entirely fresh condition. The following analysis was made from the freshest specimen obtained, as shown by its thin section:

	I.	II.
SiO_2	63.82	65.71
TiO_2	trace	
Al_2O_3	16.53	17.08
Fe_2O_3	1.28	2.84
FeO	2.93	1.79
MnO	trace	
CaO	5.57	5.24
MgO	1.99	2.57
Na_2O	4.12	3.87
K_2O	.77	1.02
H_2O	1.82	
P_2O_5	....	
CO_2	1.10	
	99.93	100.12
Sp. gr.	2.689	

I. Porphyrite from Pebbly Beach, Santa Catalina.
II. Quartz-diorite, Dognaska. (Banatite.)

The analysis of the porphyrite differs but little from that of the banatite given above. In some of its aspects the diorite is not much unlike the microscopic character of some of the banatites.

Inliers of Basement Rocks.—At a number of points in the porphyrite area, following the general direction of the main ridge to the west of Avalon, and along a line extending from the coast northwest of Avalon to near the coast east of Silver Cañon, there occur at intervals patches of the basement rocks. These are found not only along the main crest, but on several of the branch ridges to the west and northwest of Avalon, and on one of the branches running into Silver Cañon. They also occur at irregular intervals at the base of the cliffs, from Avalon Harbor for a distance of about a mile to the northwest. The outcrops along the ridges vary from a few yards to nearly 200 feet in length.

Only the largest have been indicated on the map (even those being necessarily made on a larger scale than that of the map), where they are shown as quartzite, though also including rocks from all the basement series. Those in the cliff sections occur as definite inclusions, and vary in length from a fraction of an inch to about 50 feet. The porphyrite in other places also contains inclusions, though nowhere are they so abundant as at the points mentioned.

It is possible that some of the outcrops along the ridges are remnants of a former covering to the porphyrite, but undoubtedly some (if not all) of them exist as inclusions within the igneous rock, as do the occurrences along the shore; for some of them occur in saddles along the main ridge, while those on the minor ridges are in great part hundreds of feet below the average altitude of the main ridge. To contain such large inclusions an intrusive of considerable size must be predicated. This, together with the size and form of the area of the porphyrite, points to its origin as a laccolite.[1] The microscopical character of the rock, together with its mode of occurrence, clearly indicates its intrusive nature.

The mass of the porphyrite appears to be roughly dome-shaped, with a somewhat elliptical base, and though no remnant of a cover was found it cannot be doubted that one formerly existed, now removed by extensive and active erosion. The base of the mass was not seen at any point.

Porphyrite Dikes.—Occasional dikes penetrate both the porphyrite area and that of the quartzite, the latter at the west end particularly. At the mouth of Silver Cañon the diorite, also, is cut by porphyrite dikes, one of which contains numerous inclusions of the diorite. Wherever the directions of the dikes could be determined they were found to be nearly vertical, or within 20° of the perpendicular, and approximately

---

[1] The term "laccolite" is here used in the sense of a somewhat dome-shaped mass which has been intruded into a yielding body of rock, not necessarily along the bedding planes. On this view the undisturbed condition of the beds previous to the intrusion is of minor importance, the main factors being the possession of basement and cover, and the dome-shaped form of the mass.

parallel, the range being from N. 25° E. to N. 65° E. Probably all of these dikes are of nearly the same age as the porphyrite, though many, or possibly most of them, are a little later, judging from the fact that the area of the porphyrite itself is penetrated by them. Most of the specimens obtained are very much altered, and contain a comparatively large amount of calcite, but there is enough of the original structure left to show definitely that the rocks are porphyrite. In general nothing further than this could be determined, though most of the specimens appear to be not much unlike the rocks of the main mass.

A somewhat different structure is shown in two or three of the slides, only one of which will be described. This is from a dike on the northern coast, at a point about a third of the distance from the isthmus to the extreme northwestern end of the island. The dike is nearly vertical, and has a width of eight feet. Specimens were taken from near the margin and central portion of this dike, the two being entirely different in appearance. That from near the center is a pale, even gray, while the other is a darker, mottled gray, with an intergrowth of light and dark areas. The darker parts appear to be compressed in a given plane, and, as seen with a lens, have usually a minute central cavity. The rock from the middle of the dike also contains here and there very minute thread-like cavities.

Although the hand-specimens differ so much in general appearance the contrast is not so great under the microscope. Phenocrysts are not very numerous and are wholly of labradorite, which is quite fresh. They are considerably resorbed, and seldom show crystal boundaries. The ground-mass is almost wholly filled with lath-shaped feldspar microlites of various sizes, which show a pronounced flow structure in the slide of the marginal rock, this being less noticeable in the specimen from the center. A majority of these microlites have indented terminals. In the marginal rock slide there are two distinct types of areas in the ground-mass, in both of which microlites occur, one somewhat yellowish, and the other dark in color, from minute particles contained in it. In the first type the finer portion of the ground-mass has a microcrystalline structure. In the other case the matrix is largely isotropic, and is principally of secondary silica in the form of opal. These latter areas have usually a small irregular central cavity somewhat rounded or oblong in shape. In some cases these centers have been filled with secondary quartz. These darker areas of secondary silica are usually separated from the lighter ones by an irregular and generally narrow band of a yellowish green, showing high polarization colors. Under crossed nicols and with higher powers, this is seen to be composed of finely polarizing aggregates, doubtless of some secondary ferromagnesian mineral. Similar minute, radial aggregates occur scattered through the lighter areas of the slide.

The slide from the central portion of the dike does not show the division into light and dark areas, though it contains a small amount of opaline silica and quartz. There is a larger amount of the greenish yellow ferromagnesian mineral, which is more evenly distributed through the rock, a part in the form of radial aggregates and a part as minute flakes. The matrix is cryptocrystalline, showing a feeble polarization. The ground-mass is filled with opaque, dust-like, microscopic particles.

3. Rhyolite.

Occurrence.—The rhyolite occurs in a single area, to the west of the main area of the andesite, in the Little Harbor region. It caps the summit of the ridge at this point, and extends as a light covering to the basement rocks for several hundred feet down the southern and western slopes, the underlying formations appearing here and there. At a point about midway down the western slope the rock has a roughly bedded appearance, dipping toward the west at a rather high angle. The relation of these rocks to the other igneous rocks of the island was not learned.

Macroscopic Characters.—The rhyolite varies from compact to very vesicular, and is of a light color, nearly white or with a tinge of pink. It appears to be considerably altered. It contains scattered phenocrysts of quartz (up to 3 mm. in diameter) with smaller and more numerous crystals of biotite. The vesicles indicate flow by their pronounced compression in one plane. Some of the cavities have a smooth, lustrous surface, and appear to be regular in shape, as if due to the leaching out of phenocrysts once contained in them. The form of two or three of these cavities strongly suggested a simply twinned feldspar.

Microscopic Characters.—In thin section the open-textured facies of the rock is seen to be composed largely of a dirty brown, very vesicular ground-mass, in which occur scattered phenocrysts of quartz and biotite, besides more or less magnetite in small grains or crystals. No phenocrysts of feldspar were seen, but one cavity was found which clearly had the form of a Carlsbad twin of feldspar. This cavity had a very narrow border of some secondary product strongly stained with limonite.

The quartz is in general quite clear, and occurs in idiomorphic forms which are usually more or less corroded. Frequent cracks traverse the sections. Besides brownish patches of included glass, the quartz contains occasional small spherulites, and sections of biotite partly or wholly included. No liquid inclusions were seen.

Biotite occurs in scattered, idiomorphic sections, generally with clear boundaries. A few of the rectangular sections are somewhat frayed at the ends. The crystals range in length from .15 mm. to .7 mm. The mineral exhibits the usual strong pleochroism.

The ground-mass consists in large part of feebly polarizing feldspar microlites in a dark isotropic matrix. A few of the vesicular cavities of the slides are nearly round, the rest being elliptical in form, and occasionally drawn out at the ends. Some contain a small amount of a clear, secondary mineral, and others, nearly spherical, are completely filled with almost opaque secondary products, dirty brown to black in color.

4. ANDESITE.

Occurrence.—There is one main area of the andesitic rocks with several smaller occurrences. These rocks are all, both macroscopically and microscopically, identical, and undoubtedly indicate an originally continuous area, covering the larger part of the eastern division of the island.

Ascending the ridge next the ocean, to the south of Middle Ranch Cañon, this rock is first met with at an altitude of about 300 feet, where it forms a small patch extending from this point to an elevation of about 500 feet. The next area occurs at an altitude of about 1,100 feet, where the rock not only forms the summit of this part of the ridge but caps, as well, a minor ridge which extends into the adjacent cañon. The third occurrence is near the head of this cañon. Besides these more definite areas, the soil at a number of places in this region has a purplish tinge, and the general appearance points to a more extended areal distribution of the andesite. Erosion has, however, entirely removed the rock in some places, while in others it has left only the thinnest coating on the rocks beneath, or the former covering remains simply as a coloring to the soil, in places occupied by other rocks which normally weather to a yellow.

There is a small area of andesite at the extreme southeastern end of the island. Here much of the andesite contains inclusions in varying amounts, the rock in some places being well filled with this fragmental material, which is derived in large part from earlier andesitic flows.

The main area of the andesite has a general easterly and westerly trend, and extends from the shore on the north side to the lower slopes south of Little Harbor. It reaches an extreme altitude of 2,109 feet. It consists of a series of volcanic flows which present a distinct banding on the face of the cliffs northwest and southeast of Swain's Landing. These bands have a width of four or five feet and upwards. To the east of Swain's Landing they have a dip of 10°–12° toward the Landing, while on the other side they dip in the opposite direction and at an angle of about 3°. Midway between this point and Whitley's Cove the bands are more or less irregularly flexed, though preserving a general parallelism to the shore-line.

Another small area of these rocks is found along the coast to the east of Empire Landing.

The area of andesite near the isthmus is also formed by a series of flows which show a distinct banding along the cliff on the ocean side. This banding preserves a course roughly parallel to the water-line till near Isthmus Cove, where it changes its direction, dipping at an angle of about $25°$ toward the point at the entrance to the cove, as shown in the section on the map. This formation reaches its greatest altitude near the southeastern end, where it is about 900 feet above sea-level. Along the northern shore-line of this area adjoining Isthmus Cove numerous faults are seen (not shown on the map), ranging in throw from a few inches to a hundred feet or more.

The most marked feature of this area is a distinct white band following the upper line of the cliff for some distance, and overlying the volcanic rocks. This is the bed of tuff and diatomaceous earth already mentioned as occurring with the volcanics here. That the andesite lies above as well as below it is plainly seen at a number of points. An especially good section showing the upper contact of the tuff is obtained in the little bay to the east of Isthmus Cove. Here the tuff is overlain by porous andesitic rocks.

The rocks along this part of the shore have been hollowed out in places by the force of the waves, forming caves, pillars, and blow-holes.

The coarse banding of the andesites along the cliff sections shows a variety of colors, the rocks weathering in dark grayish or purplish with occasional reddish tints. The soil formed by this series of rocks is always purplish in color, and is easily distinguished, even at a distance, from the soils which the other rocks of the island form, the latter being either reddish or yellowish.

Macroscopic Characters.—The freshest specimens of the andesite are black or nearly so. Though the rocks are in general dull, some of them have an almost greasy luster. A few of the specimens, purplish in color, appear to the eye to be fresh and compact, but with a lens it may generally be seen that they are more or less altered. Though usually compact, the rocks are vesicular in places, the irregular vesicles more or less compressed in the plane of flowage. This was noticed particularly about Isthmus Cove; also in places back of Whitley's Cove. Rarely the rock is amygdaloidal, as in the neighborhood of Whitley's Cove. The rock, though usually fracturing irregularly, at times breaks into plate-like pieces a centimeter or more in thickness. These pieces may sometimes be broken into thinner plates, owing to a laminated condition of the rock. These latter sheets vary in thickness from two millimeters to several centimeters, and their surfaces are generally yellowish from decomposition products. In other cases the rocks break into irregular masses, while showing a phenomenon similar to the foregoing in a series of fine parallel lines on those fractured surfaces at right angles to the bedding. One and only one glassy specimen of the rock was obtained, from near the small bay to the east of Isthmus Cove.

Microscopic Characters.—Microscopically the rocks, with the exception of two of the specimens examined, are pyroxene-andesites. They are usually porphyritic with a hyalopilitic ground-mass. The phenocrysts consist essentially of labradorite, augite, and hypersthene. Secondary silica is usually present in greater or less amounts. This is largely opal with occasional chalcedony. The first mineral to separate from the magma was magnetite, followed by the pyroxenes, and finally by the feldspars.

The magnetite occurs either as small octahedrons or in irregular patches, and appears to be in two generations. The largest grains are about .2 mm. in diameter. These are not very numerous. The smaller grains are more abundant, and are distributed more or less evenly through the ground-mass. These have an average diameter of about .04 mm. This scattered magnetite forms one of the most marked features of several slides which have very few phenocrysts. It amounts in one to perhaps one-third as much as the feldspars of that slide, and equals or very slightly exceeds the amount of pyroxene. The magnetite occurs as inclusions in all the other phenocrysts.

The augite is usually idiomorphic, though where not well developed as phenocrysts it occurs as minute flakes. It is very pale green, almost colorless, and without noticeable pleochroism. Its habit is prismatic and the resulting forms are generally octagonal. The crystal outlines are usually very sharp and clear, though rounded and resorbed sections are not uncommon. The cleavage, in general, is not visible except with higher powers. Cracks are common, traversing the crystal in every direction. The augites generally are remarkably clear and free from alteration products. A few of the larger sections, however, are much dulled and cracked. Twinning parallel to the orthopinacoid is common. Liquid inclusions are numerous, occasionally reaching a diameter of .02 mm. Some inclusions of magnetite also occur.

The hypersthene differs but little from the augite in general appearance, in form, habit, inclusions, or its relation to the essential minerals, and cannot always be readily distinguished from it. The former, however, is very slightly pleochroic, and all sections give parallel extinction. It has a somewhat weaker double refraction than the augite, and the interference colors of the sections are therefore in general lower, showing yellow of the first order in the majority of cases. Further, favorable sections give characteristic interference figures. Though its habit is like that of the augite, the prismatic faces occasionally are little developed, or rarely are entirely wanting. The two minerals are occasionally intergrown.

Whenever the two pyroxenes are developed as definite phenocrysts the hypersthene is always in excess of the augite. The number of the pyroxene phenocrysts in the rocks is always much smaller than that of the feldspars, the ratio being about one to four or five.

The feldspar phenocrysts occur in idiomorphic sections and are usually lath-shaped, presenting a tabular development parallel to the brachypinacoid. There is a slight tendency to the formation of ruin-like terminals. The crystal boundaries are in many cases clear and sharp, though most of them show a varying amount of resorption both on the sides and terminals of the sections, oftener the latter. Some of the feldspars clearly show a second period of growth after having been in part resorbed into the magma. Zoning is rather common. Twinning is in accordance with both albite and Carlsbad laws. Occasional cracks penetrate the sections and some of these are brought out more clearly by a staining of limonite. In sections cut approximately perpendicular to the albite lamellation the extinction angles show the species to be labradorite. As a rule the sections of the feldspar are very fresh and clear, being free from decomposition products. Inclusions are not uncommon, consisting chiefly of brownish glass with a few small and irregular pyroxenes and occasional small grains of magnetite. The glass is usually in irregular patches and is either centrally or zonally arranged. In some cases it occurs in roughly rectangular forms zonally arranged, and with their longer axis parallel to the longer axis of the crystal. The length of the sections of labradorite varies from perhaps .06 mm. to about 1.5 mm. The sections are usually quite numerous, though their number is very variable, and some of the specimens show few phenocrysts of any sort.

The phenocrysts of the various minerals generally occur as scattered crystals, but they occasionally form small aggregates. In this case, the boundaries of the feldspars yield to those of the ferromagnesian minerals with which they are in contact. This, with the occasional complete inclusion of these minerals already mentioned, shows the later development of the feldspars.

The ground-mass consists largely of feldspar microlites with a varying amount of interstitial glass. Pyroxene occurs occasionally in flakes in the ground-mass, when but little developed porphyritically. The feldspars have a low extinction angle, most of them extinguishing parallel to their length, thus placing them in the oligoclase-andesine series. Many of them appear to be simply twinned. In length they range up to about .04 mm. In nearly all cases they show a general parallelism due to flow. The amount of glass in the ground-mass is very variable, some of the slides being almost holocrystalline. In other cases the glass and secondary silica compose nearly one-half the ground-mass. This glass is readily distinguished from the opal by its color. The latter is yellowish brown and is quite clear, while the glass is dark and usually filled with small, irresolvable dots which may be magnetite.

Glassy Facies.—The glassy facies of the andesite, found as a very small occurrence near the isthmus, differs both macroscopically and microscopically from that just described. The rock is dark, almost black, and glassy, with yellowish patches scattered over the surface, the largest seen being 13 mm. in length. Occasional kaolinized feldspars occur, either within these yellowish patches or alone, up to a length of about 2 mm. With a lens very small hexagonal crystals of biotite are seen here and there. The dark ground-mass constitutes the bulk of the rock.

Under the microscope scattered and aggregated crystals of magnetite, hypersthene, augite, biotite, and feldspar are seen here and there in a glassy matrix. Magnetite, in grains and small octahedra, occurs as inclusions in the other minerals, and scattered through the ground-mass. There is only a moderate amount of biotite in the slides. It occurs as isolated idiomorphic sections, and was seen nowhere in contact with the other minerals. No basal sections were seen. The mineral everywhere exhibits the usual strong pleochroism.

Augite occurs either alone or with hypersthene, and while generally more or less rounded, it occasionally shows good crystal boundaries. It is pale green in color and non-pleochroic. One section of the augite showing rough crystal boundaries is wholly surrounded by a somewhat rectangular growth of hypersthene, the augite occupying a nearly central position. The vertical axes of the two minerals are similarly oriented. The augite is simply twinned, the two halves of the section showing a very slight difference of extinction. The hypersthene is much fractured and presents the appearance of a number of rods placed in parallel position, side by side and end to end. The interstices between the rod-like parts are filled with a brownish yellow isotropic substance closely resembling the opaline silica in the slides already described. This mineral also forms an intricate network in most of the feldspars, and constitutes a considerable proportion of many of the yellowish patches which are so numerous in the rock. These yellowish areas are largely aggregates of hypersthene and feldspar.

The hypersthene is prismatic in habit and occurs, in general, either alone or in aggregations together with occasional feldspars. The feldspar and hypersthene are the most abundant minerals of the slide, the former being somewhat in excess of the latter. The hypersthene has a pronounced pleochroism, c being light green in color, b reddish brown, and a very pale reddish. The absorption formula is $c > b > a$.

In one slide two small sections of free quartz were seen occurring quite close together and showing rounded and somewhat corroded boundaries. The sections are both crossed by numerous cracks.

The feldspars are all much resorbed, and seldom show crystal boundaries. The brownish network which most of them contain is frequently central, leaving a narrow border free from inclusions.

The ground-mass, with a high power, is seen to consist of glass filled with crystallites and microlites, with here and there perlitic cracks. With a low power the crystallites and microlites appear only as dusty particles. The perlitic cracks are distributed very irregularly, some portions of the slides being entirely free from them. They are usually quite numerous near the larger aggregates of the phenocrysts, and frequently those bordering these areas are stained yellow. Such stained cracks show, under crossed nicols, a faint polarization, as if from some radially arranged secondary product. The microlites are capillary in form, averaging .01 mm. in length, and exhibit a slight polarization. They also show a pronounced flow structure. In smaller amount are the margarites and trichites, the latter in the form of tufts and wisps, and sometimes curled at the ends. The margarites, also, are occasionally gathered into loose tufts, radiating in all directions.

Basaltic Facies.—It was stated (page 32) that the specimens examined were all pyroxene andesites, with but two exceptions. One of these was found on the minor ridge bounding the valley of Whitley's Cove on the north, not far from the contact between the basement rocks and the volcanics. The other is from the slopes to the east of Isthmus Cove. The rocks differ from those already described, in containing iddingsite.[1] The specimen from near the isthmus is dark gray in color and very much altered, but the iddingsite occurs here in good crystal forms, while in the other specimen, which is fairly fresh, the crystal boundaries show more or less resorption. As the structure of the latter rock differs considerably from that usually found in the andesites, it will be described in some detail.

The rock is purplish and compact, but passes into a black vesicular facies, apparently differing microscopically from the compact form only in the size of the component minerals and in the amount of magnetite contained. The minerals are much smaller in the vesicular portion of the specimen, and it is almost black with magnetite, in the form of grains, long, roughly bordered rods, and irregular areas. The glassy ground-mass of this portion of the rock is filled with minute black dots, doubtless magnetite. The compact portion of the specimen has very little glass, though it contains a large amount of secondary silica, chiefly in the form of opal. The rock is nearly holocrystalline, and contains

---

[1] See "Geology of Carmelo Bay," by Andrew C. Lawson. Bull. Dept. Geol., Univ. Cal., Vol. 1, pp. 31-36.

very fresh, lath-shaped feldspars in two generations, besides amber-colored iddingsite and pale green augite. The specific gravity is 2.770.

The opal has the usual appearance of that mineral macroscopically. On one face of the specimen there is a considerable crust of hyalite showing a distinctly botryoidal surface when viewed with a lens. It is colorless and nearly transparent, with a vitreous luster and a hardness of about 5.5. It is infusible, dissolving in soda, with effervescence, to a clear glass. It is in large part soluble in caustic potash, and in the closed tube gives water. The areas of opal in the slides are all isotropic. The sections readily take a stain after heating with concentrated hydrochloric acid, which, however, scarcely attacks the powdered mineral. The color of the opal in thin section is light brown. Cavities occur in it, occasionally lined with chalcedony.

Both generations of feldspars appear to be labradorite, and the larger ones form the most prominent feature of the slide, being rather numerous and of considerable size, ranging in length from about 2 mm. to 3.5 mm. They are allotriomorphic, and contain, as inclusions, considerable iddingsite, besides a little glass, an occasional smaller feldspar in the largest sections, and rarely augite. The small included feldspars always show more or less resorption.

The augite occurs in small grains with very irregular boundaries. These contain many cracks which give them a granular appearance. The mineral shows no alteration and contains as inclusions occasional grains of magnetite, besides partially included small feldspars. Several sections were seen with a few small feldspars wholly enclosed.

The most characteristic mineral of the rock is the iddingsite. In amount it slightly exceeds the augite, and equals about one-third of the feldspar. It varies in size from .06 mm. to nearly .4 mm. It was the second mineral to separate from the magma, preceded by the magnetite. It occurs as usually elongated grains with very irregular boundaries, frequently marked by bays due to magmatic corrosion.

Where the original form is indicated it is very similar to that of olivine. The form is best shown in the rock from near the isthmus. That rock, however, is very soft and much altered, and no satisfactory microscopic sections of the mineral were obtained, except for the determination of the outline. Several small but good crystals were made out in the rock, with a lens. As seen thus, the general form tallies with that described by Prof. Lawson.[1] The mineral here is deep brownish red in color, with a pronounced cleavage, the cleavage surfaces presenting a somewhat metallic luster. The central portion of the crystals is usually dark green. The forms which the slides present are of two types, both hexagonal, one with a pronounced cleavage, the other without a cleavage but with a distinct fibration at right angles to the direction of elongation. The cleavage subtends an angle, two measurements of which gave $131°$ and $133°$, respectively. Referring the mineral to the same system of axes to which Prof. Lawson has referred it, $\breve{a}$ is perpendicular to the cleavage, $\bar{b}$ in the cleavage and parallel to the fibration, $\dot{c}$ in the plane of cleavage and perpendicular to b.

The cleavage is well shown by a series of parallel and narrow, open seams, to which the extinction is in all cases parallel. In sections in which the cleavage is wanting the extinction is always parallel to the longer direction of the section and to the fibration. The latter sections show a fair biaxial interference figure. The mineral is therefore orthorhombic. The emergence of the acute bisectrix is perpendicular to the plane of cleavage and $\mathfrak{b}=\bar{b}$. The optical character of the mineral, as determined by means of the quartz wedge, is negative. $\mathfrak{a}$ is therefore the acute bisectrix, and $=\breve{a}$; $\mathfrak{c}=\dot{c}$.

The color of the mineral in thin section is very variable, especially in different parts of one and the same section, ranging from a golden brown to a clear though not bright yellow, with occasional dull greenish areas in or near the center. The deeper colors are usually marginal or along

---

[1] *Loc. cit.*

the frequent cracks, and appear to be due to limonite formed by oxidation of the contained iron. In all the attempts made, however, this color could not be leached out by acids. The deep color of the sections and strong absorption of light prevented an entirely satisfactory determination of some of the optical properties.

The pleochroism is marked in sections transverse to the cleavage, but is not so strong in sections showing no cleavage. The absorption formula is $c > b > a$. The mineral possesses a rather low mean index of refraction. In the thinner sections the iddingsite may be seen to possess a strong double refraction, though the polarization colors are usually masked by the deep color of the mineral. In sections parallel to the plane of cleavage, though the transverse fibration parallel to $\bar{b}$ is distinct, the color of the mineral conceals the fibration at right angles to this.[1]

No satisfactory material could be obtained for investigating the mineral chemically, nor was any attempt made to analyze the rock as a whole, on account of the secondary silica contained in it. One of the slides was uncovered and an attempt was made to stain the mineral. This was successful only after several trials had been made, both with concentrated and dilute acids. Dilute boiling sulphuric acid finally caused the mineral to take the stain, the results thus agreeing with those obtained by Dr. Ransome.[2]

No definite information was obtained from the Santa Catalina specimens as to the origin of this mineral. Its occurrence in a rock of this type, and possessing the form characteristic of olivine, would certainly, in the absence of any evidence to the contrary, point to the strong probability of its being a pseudomorph after that mineral. If the mineral described by Iddings[3] is the same as that under discussion—as it appears to be—it leaves little doubt on the question.

---

[1] See "The Eruptive Rocks of Point Bonita," by F. Leslie Ransome. Bull. Dept. Geol., Univ. Cal., Vol. I, No. 3, p. 91.

[2] *Loc. cit.*, p. 92.

[3] "Geology of the Eureka District, Nevada." Monograph XX, U. S. G. S., Appendix B, pp. 388–390.

Analysis.—The following analysis was made from a particularly fresh specimen of the andesite, obtained from the ridge forming the eastern boundary of the valley back of Swain's Landing:

SiO_2	61.05
TiO_2	.09
Al_2O_3	18.30
Fe_2O_3	3.49
FeO	1.11
MnO	trace
CaO	7.75
MgO	2.59
Na_2O	4.06
K_2O	1.36
H_2O	.71
P_2O_5	trace
	100.51
Sp. gr.	2.668

5. Relative Age.

The porphyrite was nowhere found in a fresh condition, while the andesite at many points is very fresh. The pronounced difference in the amount of alteration which the two rocks have undergone would suggest that the andesite is the younger. When the feldspars of the two are compared this difference amounts to more than a mere suggestion. These feldspars are closely related chemically, and, other things being equal, those of the older rock should show a greater amount of weathering. In the fresher andesite the feldspars are remarkably free from decomposition products, while those of the porphyrite always show a greater or less degree of alteration. In none of the specimens do the feldspars compare with those of the andesite in freshness.

More positive evidence as to the relative age of the two rocks was obtained on the western slopes of the andesites, in the Little Harbor region. Here, at an elevation of about 1,200 feet, numerous inclusions of the porphyrite are found in the andesite. They are of very irregular shape, averaging two or three inches in diameter. Differential weathering frequently causes them to stand out on the surface of the rock. These inclusions show beyond a doubt that the porphyrite is the older of the two rocks.

B. TUFF AND DIATOMACEOUS EARTH.

1. Occurrence.

This material has already been mentioned as occurring intercalated with the andesites of the isthmus region near their upper limits, and forming a single composite bed of considerable thickness. So far as known there is but this one occurrence. Though there are excellent exposures to the east of Isthmus Cove no complete section of the bed was seen, but from the several parts it is estimated to have a thickness of from one hundred to two hundred feet.

Besides this bed on the island, there is doubtless a considerable deposit of similar material just outside of Isthmus Cove, as indicated by the sounding contours. The large scale Coast Survey map of the isthmus emphasizes this, and shows, by mapping in the contours, a more or less continuous submarine ridge, extending out some distance. This ridge is marked in its course by a shoaling of the water at one point, and by two small islands. These islands are within the 200 ft. and 300 ft. contours, and are 29 feet and 66 feet in height, respectively. The nearer of the two is composed of tufaceous material, and the outer one is probably of the same, though it was not seen near at hand.

The bed of the island is not homogeneous but is composed of numerous minor beds of varying thickness and color, now of the white shale and now of reddish, yellowish, or dark grayish tufaceous material. The thickness of a given bed is seldom the same for any distance, and it frequently happens that a bed will wedge out and disappear within a few rods. One of the beds noted changes in thickness from about six feet to one foot in a little more than fifty feet. The various beds of the formation therefore occur in no fixed order, though the bulk of the deposits is always of the diatomaceous earth.

2. Tuff.

The tufaceous beds are not wholly of volcanic material, but contain more or less of the shale fragments, besides having occasionally a matrix of the shale (diatomaceous earth). They also contain fragments of the metamorphic material similar to that composing the underlying basement rocks. The rock as a whole is rather soft, and usually somewhat compact. One of the highest beds is made up of moderately fine angular material and is somewhat porous, as it has very little cementing material. Usually fragmental shaly material appears to form most of the finer portion of the rock. Some of the beds are more or less even-grained, composed wholly of moderately fine material, and containing nothing larger than half an inch in diameter. Others contain, besides this, large angular blocks, the largest attaining a length of about two and a half feet, though most of them are less than a foot and a half in length. By the weathering of the face of the cliffs many of these blocks project from the surface. In this way both the larger and smaller fragments gradually work out and fall to the base of the cliff. These blocks are composed almost wholly of very vesicular and usually much reddened, andesitic lava. A few large fragments of shale were seen in these coarser beds and a number of angular blocks of the metamorphic material, some of them a foot and a half in length. These beds, are in places fossiliferous, and it is said that large pectens have been found in them. No fossils were found by the writer, however.

3. Shale.

The shale wherever found is white or light gray in color, but it varies considerably in texture and composition. As a rule the rock is very soft and earthy, and can be easily scratched with the nail. In this condition it has a low specific gravity. The more earthy and less compact the rock, the more easily it splits into thin sheets. The lightest separates into paper-like fragments, almost thin enough for microscopic sections. The rock is found in two other conditions, one opaline and the other calcareous, between which and this type there are all gradations. Both these less common types are hard and compact, and are quite brittle, breaking with a conchoidal fracture. The opaline variety has a hardness of about 5, and in places has a luster like that of opal. This is No. 89, described by Dr. Hinde on page 48. The calcareous rock is somewhat darker in color than the others. It effervesces quite freely with strong acids, while with dilute acids it behaves like dolomite. The gradation of this rock into the light, earthy shale is seen by testing the different specimens with acid. The different grades of the rock show different degrees of effervescence, while the most earthy specimens give apparently none. The opaline variety does not effervesce with acid. The effervescence is due in many of the specimens to minute calcareous remains, but in the darker rock it results from the calcium-magnesium carbonate which makes up the mass of the rock. All the specimens give water in the closed tube. Heated they turn black, then white, giving off bituminous odors. The specific gravity of the earthy specimens could not be determined on account of their porous character. That of the limestone is 2.69.

No fossils of any considerable size were found in these rocks. Some of the more siliceous specimens contain minute, empty molds, arranged along the bedding planes. In one of the more compact specimens two fragmentary shell casts were seen, besides a small cast of what is probably *Tellina congesta*, Conrad. Fish-scales are quite common, with their delicate markings well preserved.

Microscopic Characters.—Under the microscope the shale is seen to consist largely of isotropic material, in which are scattered angular crystal fragments. The isotropic portions of the slides appear to be, not of glass, but wholly (or nearly so) of organic remains. The crystal fragments vary in amount in different specimens, or even in different parts of a single slide, but on the whole they form but a small percentage of the entire rock. They are largely microscopic in size, with here and there a larger fragment reaching an extreme length of about .1 mm. This fragmental material is largely of feldspar some of which shows twinning, besides an occasional dull greenish patch of chloritic material. A few quartz fragments occur, but the source of these may be the quartzite of the basement series, as several fragments were seen in one of the slides, composed of very small interlocking grains of quartz. Most of these fragmental crystals show a feeble polarization, particularly the smaller ones. In one of the slides were seen several larger fragments of andesite, somewhat altered, but still fresh enough to show the twinning of the porphyritic feldspars.

A section of the calcareous rock shows that it is apparently free from the angular fragments of the shaly specimens, while, as before, the mass of the rock appears to consist of organic remains. With crossed nicols the larger molds are seen to be filled with calcite. The ground-mass of the rock is not isotropic, but gives the delicate polarization tints of calcite. With a high power the entire rock is seen to have a microcrystalline structure, being made up of irregular grains of calcite. This structure bears no relation to the distribution of the organic material in the rock, except in the case of the Foraminifera.

Character of the Organic Remains.—A number of small fragments of the shale were forwarded by Prof. Lawson to Dr. George J. Hinde for examination. He has kindly placed his conclusions at Prof. Lawson's disposal, in the following note.

"From small samples of these rocks sent over to me by Prof. A. C. Lawson I have prepared thin microscopic sections where the material was sufficiently coherent to allow of such being made, and in the case of the very soft rocks the fine powder has been mounted just as it occurs, without washing away the finer débris. I have only aimed in the following notes at giving a general idea of the nature of the organisms of which the rocks are composed, for the task of recognizing even the genera present would prove too long and difficult to be undertaken, and moreover, the material at hand, though sufficient to show the general character of the organisms, would not be enough for determination of particular forms.

"No. 90. This soft, white, earthy rock is essentially diatomic in character. Both in section and in powder it is seen to consist of a mass of heterogeneously mingled fragments of diatom frustules, with a small proportion of complete forms. By far the larger mass of the rock is formed by the broken up and disintegrated particles of the diatoms, and the smallest and finest portions recognizable under the microscope are clearly organic débris. *Coscinodiscus* appears to be the predominant genus. Detached sponge spicules are fairly numerous. They are principally pin-shaped and styliform; also a few simple fusiform rods occur belonging to the Monactinellid division of siliceous sponges. The Tetractinellid sponges are represented by a few fragmentary trifid spicules and globate forms. Only one or two somewhat doubtful fragments of Radiolaria were noticed, and these organisms must have been very sparsely present, for their structures are stouter and more capable of preservation than the diatoms. The silica of these organisms—diatoms and sponges—appears to be unaltered in the fossilization—it retains the same glassy aspect as in recent examples. In addition to the siliceous organisms, Foraminifera are likewise present, and they yet retain the calcareous structure of their walls, though hardly so well preserved as in the case of the siliceous fossils. A rather large form of *Textularia* is the most common of the Foraminifera. It is to these organisms that the calcareous portions of the rock are due. The rock is very finely laminated, showing a series of well marked undisturbed layers of organic remains in which are scattered some minute angular chips of minerals here and there.

"No. 118. A whitish, comparatively soft, earthy rock. Examined both in section and in powder. Very similar to the preceding in consisting nearly wholly of diatoms and diatomic débris. *Coscinodiscus* is very numerous; some forms relatively large. Sponge spicules are also present, but I could not certainly distinguish any Radiolaria. No Foraminifera to be seen in this specimen, and there was no reaction of the rock in acid. It is not unlikely that the calcareous organisms have been leached away, for minute empty pores can be seen in transverse sections of the beds. It has a lesser proportion of angular rock chips than the preceding (No. 90).

"No. 147. Very soft, earthy white rock, readily breaking up into fine flaky laminæ. No reaction in acid. Like the preceding this is also nearly entirely a diatomic rock, but the diatoms are here of different forms, *Melosira?* and *Grammatophora* being most conspicuous. There are fair numbers of sponge spicules, usually broken; they are chiefly pin-shaped and styliform. Neither Foraminifera nor Radiolaria were recognizable in the material examined. The angular rock chips were fewer in this rock than in the previous specimens (90 and 118).

"No. 152.[1] A pale gray, hard rock—just scratches with knife—compact, flinty fracture, readily effervesces in acid. Examined in section only. It consists, like the soft rock above referred to (No. 90), mainly of diatoms and diatomic débris; the ground-mass of the rock is, as far as can be seen under the microscope, wholly of the broken up diatom frustules. Both the minute fragments and the entire forms are as unchanged as in the soft rocks. *Coscinodiscus* is abundant, also *Navicula*, *Grammatophora* and other forms. Some of the spaces between the diatom frustules have been infilled with calcite. There are a few Radiolaria present, spheroidal and discoidal forms, but their numbers are insignificant in comparison with the diatoms. Sponge spicules are apparently absent. Foraminifera are fairly common and well preserved, showing their wall structures; the most abundant is a large species of *Textularia*, probably the same form as that in No. 90. The interiors of the Foraminifera have been infilled with calcite. Angular chips hardly to be seen in the sections of this rock.

---

[1] No. 152 is the limestone, the analysis of which is given later, p. 50.

"No. 89. Pale gray or cream-tinted hard rock—just scratches with knife—no action in acid. The section examined showed numerous minute pores, but whether these indicated spaces where organisms had been is doubtful. No organisms could be recognized in this rock, which, nevertheless, appears to be of opalized silica. A few angular chips could be distinguished in polarized light.

"With the exception of this last specimen, the siliceous and silico-calcareous rocks of the island of Santa Catalina are remarkable for the very slight amount of alteration which the structures of the siliceous and calcareous organisms have undergone in the fossilization. Both the most delicate diatoms and the Foraminifera occur in these beds together, in nearly as well preserved condition as in deposits now forming. The beds may well be compared with recent diatomic oozes, and, as in these latter, there is a small percentage of sponge spicules, Radiolaria and Foraminifera mingled with the prevailing diatoms. The paucity of Radiolaria in the beds is a peculiar feature. Sections of these rocks show very distinctly that the entire material, down to the smallest particles, is of organic remains mostly now broken up, for the proportion of perfect forms is small compared with the large quantity of fragmental débris. The amount of the foreign angular mineral particles is insignificant."

Chemical Characters.—This note would seem to leave no room for question as to the organic origin of the shale, but that the point might be considered from all sides, a chemical determination was made of the amount of soluble silica in the most earthy and least calcareous of the specimens. About a a gram of the roughly powdered material was used, in a ten per cent. solution of potassium hydrate. For the purpose of comparison specimens of pumice and nearly pure volcanic ash were taken and subjected to the same treatment as the shale. All the material was well dried at 100° (C) before weighing and adding to the solution. The solutions were brought to boiling twice, being allowed to stand some hours in the interval, and for about a day after the second heating.

The residues were then filtered off, and the silica was precipitated in the filtrate by acidifying with hydrochloric acid, and evaporating to dryness. The weight of the silica obtained by this process was compared with the weight of the residues, and except for the shale they all tallied very closely. All lost some silica, and on the addition of ammonia after the precipitation of the silica a slight amount of alumina was precipitated in all the solutions, showing that the alumina in the rock was acted on to some extent. The same test applied to the potassium hydrate (which occasionally contains alumina) gave no precipitate. The results showed that the pumice had lost 3.2 per cent. of silica, the volcanic ash 4.2 per cent., while the shale had lost 70.3 per cent. The powdered residue from this shale was subjected to microscopic examination, and with the higher powers was found to contain a large percentage of minute crystalline fragments. Nothing could be made of the isotropic material of the residue. A considerable amount of the residue thrown into dilute acid produces momentary effervescence, showing that a part of it is calcareous, doubtless organic remains.

Origin of the Shale.—These results show that the shale is largely composed of opaline silica, and, together with the statement of Dr. Hinde, are sufficient to disprove, for this region at least, the hypothesis tentatively advanced by Prof. Lawson[1] that the Miocene shale of the coast of California is largely of volcanic origin. That this shale is a part of the same Miocene shale which is found so extensively developed along the coast, there can be little doubt, although the proof obtained is not positive. It has a similar appearance, presents the same variations, contains abundant micro-organisms (a characteristic feature of the Miocene shales), while the occurrence of fish scales adds another link to the chain of evidence, as this is another marked characteristic of the coastal shales. Further, the Miocene shale occurs at San

---

[1] "The Geology of Carmelo Bay," by Andrew C. Lawson. Bull. Dept. Geol., Univ. Cal., Vol. 1, pp. 24-26.

Clemente Island, some twenty-five miles further south. If, then, these deposits are a part of the extensive Miocene shales, we cannot consider their development as in any way local, or as influenced by the deposits with which they are associated, for the conditions favorable for the development of the micro-organisms of the shale at that time must have been far reaching. Except for the few microscopic fragments, the shale as it occurs here is in general peculiarly free from the tufaceous material with which it is associated, indicating a considerable interval of quiet deposit, interrupted at times by violent local volcanic outbursts. Santa Catalina at this time was an island, as now, though doubtless separated from the mainland by a considerably greater expanse of water. The true relative attitude of island and mainland and the intermediate channel can be revealed only from the neighboring coastal formations. In addition to other evidence, the porous character of some of the lavas associated with the tuff and diatomaceous earth, and the remains of large pectens found in the tuff, indicate that these deposits could not have been formed in abyssal depths. It would appear from other reasons that they were laid down in not more than 600 or 1,000 feet of water.

Analysis of Limestone.—For the purpose of ascertaining the character of the limestone, a partial analysis was made by dissolving fragments in acid, and determining the amount of the constituents in the solution thus obtained. The results were as follows:

Insoluble residue	8.234
Al_2O_3 Fe_2O_3 (a little)	2.862
CaO	27.944
MgO	13.012
Ignition and CO_2	43.615

No determination of the alkalies was made. A qualitative examination was made for phosphoric acid, but no quantitative determination, though considerable was found to be present. The residue in this case also was examined microscopically. While the slide of the rock showed no fragmental material, this powder showed a very few scattered mineral fragments here and there, but even in this concentrated form they are not so numerous as in the slides of the shaly specimens. Aside from these the residue is wholly isotropic and consists largely of the remains of diatoms, with occasional Radiolaria. It is interesting to note, in comparing the chemical and microscopical characters of the rock, what a small percentage of organic remains is necessary to give a slide the appearance of being well filled with them.

The results thus show that the rock is a magnesian limestone. Without doubt the carbonates are original and not secondary, their source probably being the sea-water in which the organic forms were laid down.

C. SEDIMENTARY DEPOSITS.

Besides the beds at the isthmus, two minor deposits of sedimentary material were found, both within the main area of the andesite. One occurs in a saddle on the principal ridge to the west of Orizaba, at a distance of not more than a mile; the other, shown by a dotted surface on the map, is on the lower slopes of the andesite in the Little Harbor region.

The first mentioned is only a small deposit in the lowest part of the saddle, extending not more than five or six feet up the slope on either side. The rock which forms the deposit proper is more or less open and is composed almost wholly of coarse shell fragments roughly cemented with secondary calcite. These fragments, though too small for a specific determination, appear to be the remains of large pectens. In addition to this, there were seen a number of rolled pebbles of andesite and porphyrite, and several large blocks of a white earthy material, all of which appear to have been deposited here. It is possible, however, that they were brought here by the Indians who formerly occupied the island, since there is unmistakable evidence that this saddle was one of their camping grounds. The specimens from the earthy blocks show a free effervescence with dilute acid, and contain in places rough, free, calcite crystals, several millimeters in diameter.

The lower slopes of the andesite in the Little Harbor region, up to an altitude of six or seven hundred feet, are everywhere strewn with rolled pebbles of andesite, porphyrite, and quartzite. Near the northern border of these lower levels there are two small deposits of white, earthy material. Along the southern border, on the ridge adjoining Middle Ranch Cañon, there is a considerable deposit of sandstone and conglomerate, and a little above this on the same slope another deposit of the earthy material. All the specimens of the latter rock wherever found effervesce freely with dilute acid. A very few rough shell casts were found in one of the areas of the earthy rock. The rock powder under the microscope showed no organic remains. The bulk of the powder gives the high polarization colors of calcite. Some of the specimens contain occasional small pebbles. In the coarser deposits there are all gradations, from conglomerate, with pebbles averaging one-half an inch in diameter, to a fine-grained, yellowish, micaceous sandstone. None of these effervesce with acids. A search for fossils revealed a few indeterminable shell-casts. These deposits of sandstone and conglomerate are in general thin, though at one point they reach a thickness of about fifteen feet.

D. BRECCIA.

Beginning near the extreme southeastern point of the island, and extending along the coast to the northward, is a small area of quartzite breccia. As seen in the gulches it is, in part at least, bedded, the beds varying in the coarseness or fineness of their material. The coarser beds contain occasional large blocks two feet or more in diameter, and, rarely, reaching a length of several yards. The material composing this breccia, so far as can be made out with a lens, is wholly quartzite, except for occasional blocks and fragments of andesite seen near the upper part of the series. The bedding of the breccia is seen on the upper part of the cliffs at the northern end of the area as a rather coarse banding, approximately parallel to the shore-line. Toward the south the banding becomes somewhat irregular and is lost to view some time before the extreme point is reached. Here the breccia is seen at the base of the cliffs, and so far as could be determined it is, in part at least, included in the porphyrite (see Plate III, fig. 1) which occurs here on the cliffs just above.

This porphyrite is a white, much weathered rock, and it is possible that it occurs here as a dike of considerable size, or as an intrusive sheet, and does not belong to the main occurrence of this rock. At any rate it is in some respects unlike the porphyrite as it usually occurs. Within the area just described the porphyrite outcrops along the shore at one other point, at least, where the rock is to all appearances like that of the main area. The breccia at the point of the island is cut by a dike of greenish porphyrite about two feet wide, which also cuts the white porphyrite mentioned above.

About midway between Pebbly Beach and the extremity of the island there is a small beach at the base of the cliffs, which is partly made up of boulders and smaller masses of a conglomerate resembling the breccia in the material of which it is composed. This has apparently fallen from the cliffs above, although no rounded material was anywhere seen in place by the writer. So far as observed, these boulders are composed of water-worn metamorphic pebbles, imbedded in a large amount of compact, greenish cement. This cement shows a marked effervescence with dilute acid, and under the microscope it is seen to be composed in large part of angular fragments of quartz and quartzite, in a thin cement which is largely calcite. Several small sections were seen, closely resembling the porphyrite in appearance, and containing porphyritic feldspars, but much altered by decomposition products.

The observations made were too limited to prove conclusively the relations of the breccia to the main body of the porphyrite and to the andesite, but some of the evidence points to the probability of its being older than either.

E. BASEMENT SERIES.

In surface area the rocks of the basement series cover a little more than half the island. They consist mainly of quartzites and mica-schists, with several smaller areas of talc- and amphibole-schists and serpentine.

The occurrences of the other basement rocks within the quartzite area were not exactly mapped, and for that reason they appear on the map without definite boundaries. The actinolite areas, in particular, are more extensive than is here indicated. The main occurrences of these rocks are as indicated, but smaller areas of all of them occur elsewhere within the quartzite area. The actinolite-schists, besides their main occurrence, are found in the area of the quartzite about Middle Ranch Cañon. The areas of the basement rocks found within the porphyrite area northwest of Avalon are in part of actinolite- and talc-schists, with some serpentine. Talc-schist is also found near the center of the west end, toward the northern coast. Besides the serpentine areas mapped, a small patch was found on the ridge to the south of Middle Ranch Cañon, and another not far from the extreme northwestern point of the island. A patch of garnet amphibolite is found just to the west of the border of the andesite in the Little Harbor region.

I. QUARTZITE.

The quartzite occurs distinctly bedded, and wherever it was possible observations for dip and strike were made, though these were insufficient to warrant a statement with regard to the beds as a whole. In many places these readings give no real indication of the general dip and strike of the series, owing to local folding with minor plications, and to occasional faulting. By a comparison of the various readings made, however, the western division of the island appears to have a synclinal structure. Whether this is true for the division to the southeast of the isthmus cannot be stated.

An excellent cliff section showing the general stratification is seen on the southern coast of the west end, where the bedding is distinctly visible for three or four miles along the shore. For the greater part of the distance the dip of the beds is quite uniform, though the minor beds and sheets observed show intricate folding and crumpling. The dip ranges from S. 15° E. to S. 45° E., at an angle varying from 15° to about 30°.

On the northern coast of this part of the island the dip, so far as observed, is northerly, and varies considerably in amount, the average lying between 25° and 50°. A characteristic section of the bedding is shown in Plate III, fig. 1, a view of the shore at the north end of the beach of Cherry Valley, the second small bay to the north of Isthmus Cove.

The quartzites are nearly everywhere intersected by numerous veins of secondary quartz, usually of small size and running in various directions. In places, however, these veins attain a width of a foot or more. At a number of points some of the veins contain a small percentage of mineral ores.

The quartzite is usually bedded in thin and more or less irregular sheets. They range from a fraction of an inch to two or three inches in thickness, averaging perhaps half an inch. These sheets are usually separated by partings of a dark earthy character, varying in thickness from the thinnest film to about a quarter of an inch. In the more thinly bedded quartzite these partings are frequently thicker than the quartzite sheets.

Macroscopic Characters.—The quartzite is occasionally milky white; usually, however, as seen with a lens, it appears colorless and glassy. Rarely it is found black, while here and there it occurs with a tinge of pink, or even considerably reddened, owing to the presence of minute garnets, either scattered through the sheet or arranged in bands parallel to the bedding. Many of these quartzite sheets appear to be wholly free from mica, the surface of the sheet glistening from the minute quartz crystals composing the rock. Other specimens, in cross-section, appear to be of clear quartz, but when viewed in the plane of the bedding numerous minute scales of muscovite are seen scattered over the surface. In all fractured surfaces these flakes are seen to be arranged with their planes parallel to the plane of the bedding. There are all gradations between this and specimens in which the mica is the most prominent mineral.

The layers which form the partings of the quartzite beds are quite dark, varying from a dark gray to a yellowish or reddish color due to iron stain. They are finely schistose and readily flake off; are quite soft and have usually a smooth, silvery surface. Even where this silvery luster is not at first apparent it may easily be made out with a lens. The layers appear to be composed of mica or its decomposition products. Tested chemically the mineral shows the presence of a large amount of alumina, a little iron, no lime and a little magnesia, besides giving a decided flame reaction for potassium. The optical characters of the flakes could not be determined, owing to their want of transparency.

A considerable proportion of the rocks of the west end have much the appearance of gray sandstone to the unaided eye, though with a lens they are seen to be composed largely of this micaceous material, with minute lenses or grains of the quartzite scattered through it. These micaschists occur indiscriminately with the rocks which are more properly quartzites, and occasionally lens-shaped masses of the quartzite are found in such areas. There are all gradations between these rocks in which the mica is predominant and those in which the quartz predominates.

Besides the micaceous partings of the quartzites there were found at a number of points partings of blue amphibole, having frequently a silky luster. This amphibole also occurs in larger masses in a schistose condition. The occurrences of this rock were not mapped, but they are found particularly in the Little Harbor region, apparently confined to the neighborhood of the areas of the amphibole- and talc-schists and serpentine. It is probable that here, as elsewhere in California, these blue amphibole-schists are due to local contact metamorphism occasioned by the intrusion of basic irruptives.[1]

Microscopic Characters.—Only one slide was made of the quartzites, which, however, is doubtless typical of the purer quartzites in general. It consists almost entirely of a mosaic of clear quartz grains of irregular shape and size. Many of them are flattened in a direction parallel to the plane of schistosity, thus giving frequently very much elongated sections. Their boundaries interlock in an extremely intricate manner. Occasional pale pink garnets occur as inclusions in the quartz, averaging a little less than .1 mm. in diameter. They are for the most part rounded, though two or three present crystal boundaries. Long narrow sections of what is probably sillimanite are comparatively numerous, nearly all arranged with their longer axes parallel to the plane of schistosity or to the direction of the flattening of the quartz grains. The terminals taper more or less gradually to a point. No cross-sections were seen. The mineral is colorless and has a moderately high index of refraction, somewhat higher than that of quartz, and it may therefore be readily distinguished from the latter in ordinary light. The double refraction is considerable, giving brilliant, though somewhat mottled, polarization colors. The extinction is in all cases parallel and perpendicular to the longer axis of the mineral. In all the sections observed the longer axis is the axis of less elasticity as shown by the quartz wedge. No optical figure was obtained.

---

[1] "A Contribution to the Geology of the Coast Ranges," by Andrew C. Lawson. Am. Geol., Vol. XV (June, 1895), p. 352.
"The Geology of Angel Island," by F. Leslie Ransome. Bull. Dept. Geol., Univ. Cal., Vol. 1, No 7.

2. Actinolite and Hornblende Schists.

The actinolite-schist occurs bedded, showing greater variation than the quartzite in the thickness of the beds. It also frequently exhibits plications such as occur in the quartzite. Some of these schists occur in rather thin beds, with a finely schistose structure, the slender needles of actinolite parallel to the plane of schistosity. In other cases, especially the coarser forms of the rock, it is found showing no marked schistose arrangement. The crystals in these coarser schists frequently have a length of three or four centimeters. The rocks are more or less compact, and in general are composed of columnar or acicular actinolite crystals, but always associated with a greater or less amount of other minerals. The most common mineral accompanying the actinolite is talc. This is usually in small amounts, but rarely it becomes the dominant mineral, forming a matrix in which the needles of actinolite are embedded. Chlorite occasionally occurs with the actinolite, and like the talc, this sometimes, though rarely, becomes dominant. The chlorite varies in occurrence from minute flakes to plates several centimeters in diameter. A small amount of quartz is frequently found in these schists, and occasionally both quartz and feldspar, in varying amounts, occur associated with the actinolite and hornblende.

Almost the entire area of actinolite- and hornblende-schist is composed of the former. The latter is confined to the area which contains the serpentine, occurring here with the actinolite-schist. The rocks are coarse-grained, compact, greenish black in color, and are composed of coarsely prismatic crystalline hornblende. A small amount of mica is occasionally associated with it.

3. Serpentine.

The serpentine of this same area is found on the summits of these hills of amphibole-schist. The hills are in the neighborhood of 1,000 feet in height, and the serpentine which outcrops here is two or three hundred feet in thickness. It occurs stratiform, with an average dip of from 20° to 30° in a northerly direction. The rocks are very hard and compact, and in weathering present an extremely rough surface, with projecting fragments, many of which have sharp, jagged points. It is doubtless owing to this bold, irregular surface that one of these hills has received the name of Granite Peak. The surface of this rock is also irregularly pitted. The occurences are almost wholly of this facies, and little evidence was seen of internal movement, causing a slickensided appearance. The general appearance of the rock in the field is in most respects quite unlike that of the serpentine of the Potrero, San Francisco, described by Dr. Palache,[1] which is typical of much of the serpentine of the Coast Range. There are a few small patches of magnesite within the serpentine area. The hand-specimens of the serpentine vary in color from a dirty greenish white to a dark bluish green, more or less mottled with limonite. The compact specimens show an indistinctly banded structure, and have a rather uneven fracture. This surface is entirely different from the smooth and somewhat polished surface of the pale green, slickensided specimens. Traversing the surface in lines approximately parallel to the banding are occasional fine veins and threads of chrysotile, with their fibres at right angles to the enclosing walls, and stained here and there with iron. More numerous and finer threads cross the surface at right angles to the larger veins, and nearly all are stained with limonite. Threads of magnetite run through the rock, in no fixed direction. In some places the rocks contain many minute veins of secondary silica, running at right angles to the banding. Cross-sections seen on the surface show that they are filled with the silica arranged in concentric rings. No remnants of the minerals from which the serpentine was derived were seen in any of the specimens, but it doubtless consisted in large part of olivine, for the mesh-structure characteristic of the serpen-

---

[1] "The Lherzolite-Serpentine and Associated Rocks of the Potrero, San Francisco." Bull. Dept. Geol., Univ. Cal., Vol. 1, No. 5, pp. 161-179.

tines so derived is seen throughout the greater part of the slides.

Areas of a somewhat different facies of the serpentine occur within the talc and garnet-amphibolite area. This rock is hard, compact, occurring massive, and not stratiform. As in the serpentines just described, minute veins of silky chrysotile traverse it here and there. The rock is very dark green, and scattered through it are aggregates of a magnesian mineral, with pearly luster, whose optical properties were not investigated. Besides this mineral, there occurs in various amounts, associated with the compact serpentine, a pale green, lamellar mineral with the optical properties of bastite.

4. Talc-Schist.

The area in which this serpentine is found is largely of talc-schist, usually found as a soft, foliated rock, stained yellow with limonite. It has a silvery luster, and when looked at closely the talc is seen to be of a pale green color. It is quite smooth, with a greasy feel, and is easily scratched with the nail. The rock splits readily along the schistose surfaces. Near the western end of the area, back of Empire Landing, there is a soapstone quarry where is found a facies of the schist, which but little resembles the foliated form just described. This is massive, not schistose, and has a dark gray color with a tinge of green. The rock may be scratched with the nail only in places, showing that it is not wholly talc. The chief difference between this rock and the foliated schist is the presence everywhere through it of a mineral with a pronounced lamellar structure, occurring in moderately small, bladed forms, which are interlaced in all directions. This mineral appears to be the chief constituent of the rock, and at least equal to the talc in amount. It is pale green in color, with a metalloidal luster, and a hardness of about 4. Before the blowpipe it gives the characteristic reactions of serpentine. With a lens the silvery flakes of talc may be seen here and there, besides scattered grains of pyrite.

Under the microscope the rock is seen to be composed in part of an allotriomorphic aggregate of bastite, and partly of irregular areas of talc, with several small patches of magnesite. Small amounts of pyrite are scattered through the slide.

The bastite occurs in plates or somewhat lath-shaped forms, and is colorless or with the faintest tinge of green. The mineral is non-pleochroic, even in moderately thick cleavage flakes. It has a pronounced fibration parallel to the vertical axis. Its extinction is characteristic of a rhombic mineral, being in all cases parallel to this fibration. It has a low index of refraction, and gives low interference colors, much like those of feldspar. The cleavage flakes show the fibration which is observed in thin section. Rarely a needle of pyrite is seen in the fibration. Cleavage flakes give a good biaxial interference figure, and show that the plane of the optical axes is at right angles to the plane of cleavage and parallel to the fibration. The optical character of the mineral is negative, as determined both by the mica plate and quartz wedge. The bastite is everywhere altering to talc, and all stages of the process may be seen. Alteration begins along the margin and along the cleavage planes, and works inward. Occasionally the talc occurs as a pseudomorph after the bastite, giving a parallel extinction, owing to a parallel arrangement of the fibres of the talc. Usually, however, the talc occurs in patches of irregular shape, and without a definite extinction throughout an entire revolution of the stage, owing to the compensatory effect of the irregularly oriented talc fibres.

5. Origin of the Serpentines.

No detailed petrographical study was made of the serpentine rocks of the island, but such as was made proves them to be variable in their microscopic structure, and therefore different in their origin. At no point was there seen any of the unaltered rock from which the serpentine was derived, so that the conclusions must be drawn from the microscopic structure of the serpentine itself. Judging from this, the serpentines may be roughly divided into three groups according to their probable origin: (1) those derived from pyroxenites, (2) those from rocks composed largely of olivine, and (3) those from a rock in which both rhombic pyroxene and olivine were among the essential constituents. The first are now characterized by the bastite structure, the second by the mesh-structure. It is probable that the whole of the talc-schist is derived from the first form of serpentine.

6. Garnet-Amphibolite.

Along the ridge near the upper limit of the talc-schists, and within that area, are found here and there small, projecting bosses, with occasional larger areas, of garnet-amphibolite. This rock usually presents a somewhat roughened surface, more or less reddened with iron oxide. It is not compact, and readily crumbles under the hammer. The fresher material is dark or almost black in color, and appears to be composed wholly of a brownish or greenish hornblende, with roughly rounded red garnets in varying size and amount. In some places these garnets attain a diameter of about 3 mm. and form the principal feature of the rock, while in other cases the rock is composed almost entirely of a somewhat fine-grained hornblende, and an occasional minute garnet may be made out only with the aid of a lens. At a few points the rock occurs as a black, rather coarsely granular aggregate, composed entirely of hornblende, so far as can be determined with a lens.

A slide was made of the facies of the rock containing the largest garnets. There are nine of these garnets in the slide, ranging from 2 to 3 mm. in diameter. Microscopically the rock is composed of scattered, pale pink garnets in a matrix of hornblende. Here and there are small grains of rutile. The hornblende is brownish with a tinge of green, and occurs in allotriomorphic plates, with seldom a hint of crystallographic form. The boundaries are usually well marked by a limonite stain. The sections themselves are quite fresh and free from products of decomposition. The mineral has a pronounced prismatic cleavage. It is quite strongly pleochroic, c being dark, greenish brown, b deep, yellowish brown, and a very pale, brownish green. The absorption scheme is $c \gtreqqless b > a$. Inclusions are common, and in many of the sections abundant. They are largely minute flakes of a mineral with low polarization colors, and a refractive index somewhat higher than that of the hornblende. The same mineral occurs in scattered flakes in the garnets also, and they are there seen to be colorless or nearly so. In the hornblende these flakes are in small, open areas, usually collected near the center of the including crystal. Besides these inclusions, occasional small grains of rutile are found.

The rutile, in general, through the slide, occurs as rounded and usually oblong grains, in color deep yellowish to reddish brown, varying with the tints of amber. These grains are usually found along the lines which mark the boundaries between the hornblendes, and generally several together occur along the same line. They have an extremely high index of refraction, and on account of the consequent diffusion of light the extinctions are not sharp and clear. The direction of extinction in the grains which are distinctly elongated is parallel and at right angles to the axis of elongation. The mineral shows a pronounced though not strong pleochroism, and has a strong absorption. As the grains could not be distinguished from the dark hornblende in the crushed rock, the hornblende was dissolved out by means of hydrofluoric acid, when the minute, dark grains of the rutile could be readily distinguished from the pale red fragments of garnet, neither of these being attacked by the acid. Some of these grains were then separated and tested for titanium, with favorable results.

The garnets have quite irregular boundaries, and along the margin are frequently intergrown with the hornblendes which surround them. In a number of cases minute fragments of the garnets are completely enclosed by the bordering hornblendes, while occasionally a fragment of hornblende is wholly surrounded by the garnet near its margin. Frequent cracks, many of them iron-stained, intersect the garnets, without definite direction. Macroscopically the garnets appear to have a zonal structure, with a narrow and somewhat clouded outer zone, a broad middle zone, seemingly of the clear pink garnet, and a slightly darker inner zone. Under the microscope this structure is seen to be due to inclusions in the garnet. With crossed nicols the sections are, as a whole, not perfectly isotropic, but transmit a faint light in all positions. This is due to a multitude of microscopic, dust-like inclusions, which fill the central portions of the garnets. With higher powers these inclusions cannot be resolved, but are seen to be of some rather brightly polarizing mineral. They do not always occur in solid areas, for portions of the space are free from them, these isotropic portions running like veins through the mass. These areas fill the greater part of the sections, but there is always a narrow, irregular band along the margin which is free from these minute inclusions, and is isotropic under crossed nicols. The darker, central areas appear to be due to a clouding, the nature of which could not be determined. Besides these minute inclusions there are others scattered through the slide, which have been mentioned in connection with the hornblende. Some of the garnets contain here and there, particularly along the isotropic borders, minute needles of a yellowish to brownish mineral, with parallel extinction and high refractive index, and giving high polarization colors. This mineral is probably rutile. A few of these needles were seen in some of the hornblendes bordering the garnets in which the inclusions are found, and some of the needles were seen extending from the one mineral into the other. There are rarely inclusions of large grains of rutile and small hornblendes.

IV. GEOMORPHOGENY.

1. SUBMARINE TOPOGRAPHY.

The submarine contours surrounding the island have been represented for depths of 200, 300, 400 and 600 feet. The discussion of the results arrived at by a study of this feature of the topography has been left till this point, as these results are so closely connected with the geological history of the island. By mapping in the deeper contours, it is seen that the general form of the island is preserved to a depth of at least 1,800 feet, and doubtless somewhat beyond this, though the indications are that the pronounced trench outside Little Harbor gradually loses its character, so that at some greater depth the outline of the entire mass may be much simpler.

In looking at the map it will be noticed that the average distance from the shore to the 200 feet contour is much less than the average distance from the 200 feet to the 400 feet contour. This is particularly marked in those parts of the island where the cliff cutting is the most rapid. By mapping in the contours on the large Coast Survey map of the isthmus these features are strikingly brought out. Here, since there is more detail, it is readily seen that the more rapid deepening of the water near the shore extends to about 250 feet, and to this level the details of the present outline are fairly well preserved. Beyond the 250 feet contour there is a broad platform with a very gentle outward slope (of about $1°$) to some point beyond the 300 feet level.

Beyond the 400 feet contour the water deepens rapidly on the southern side of the island, while on the north the widely separated contours indicate a gradual slope. The pronounced difference between the two sides is well shown in the accompanying sections (figs. 5 and 6), which were chosen as most fairly representing the average character of the two sides respectively. The first is the section along a line at right angles to the outermost point north of Whitley's Cove; the other, along a line at right angles to the shore on the opposite side of the island, at a point to the southwest of the most southern occurrence of the andesite on the map. These sections suggest the possible origin of the island as a tilted orographic block, the rapid descent on the southern side contrasting strongly with the moderate slope on the other. The contrast is similar to that of sections taken on opposite sides of San Clemente Island which is almost certainly such a block.[1] The platform mentioned

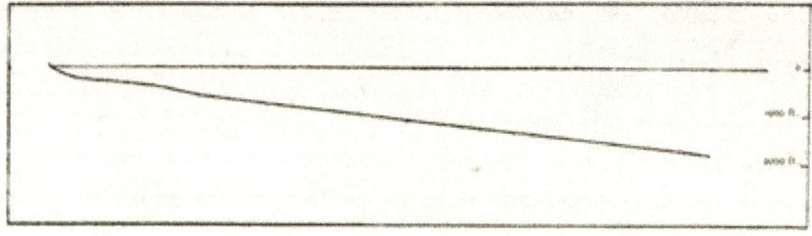

FIGURE 5—Submarine profile, north side of Santa Catalina.

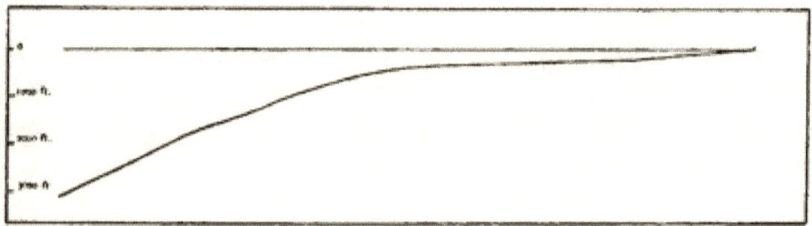

FIGURE 6—Submarine profile, south side of Santa Catalina.

as occurring above the 350 feet contour is well brought out in the section from the southern side, though the slight increase in slope above the 200 feet contour is not marked. The features make it clear that before the present sinking of the island began it stood some 350 feet higher than now. That this platform is later than the andesite is seen from the fact that it has been cut in the tufaceous deposits at the isthmus. The island stood for some time at or near that level, while rapid cutting was going on both along the cliffs on the most exposed sides, and in the softer tufaceous deposits near the isthmus, where the erosion of the harder rocks is comparatively slow. When the island had been

---

[1] "The Post-Pliocene Diastrophism of the Coast of Southern California," by Andrew C. Lawson. Bull. Dept. Geol., Univ. Cal., Vol. 1, No. 4, p. 129.

reduced to the form approximately shown by the 200 feet contour the present sinking began. This is shown not only by the increase of the submarine slope, but also in the isthmus chart, by the preservation of the main features of the present drainage system, showing that the recent stream-valley flooding took place at that level. The information on this point obtained from this latter source, however, is reliable only within certain limits, as a rapid, partial or complete filling up of these sunken channels in their lower levels might easily cause an error in the interpretation of the facts. But, taken in connection with the other evidence, they may be considered as trustworthy to a certain extent at least.

2. Outline of History.

The alteration and deformation of the basement rocks of Santa Catalina probably took place before the individualization of the mass now forming the island. In the opinion of the writer, the history of Santa Catalina began with the tilting of an orographic block formed of the already altered basement rocks. This view is based on the character of the submarine contours and the slight recent tilting shown in the slope of the summits (see figs. 2 and 3, page 7). The tilting was no doubt gradual, and has continued intermittently to comparatively recent times. This is shown in connection with the figures just referred to, as it was pointed out that the angle of the slope of the crest is about $1°$ from the horizontal, and in the direction of tilting toward the north. No further evidence of the original crust-block is seen on the land, owing to the extensive erosion to which the mass has since been subjected.

The time of the original tilting is not known, but the crust-block must have been at that time a part of the mainland. By long continued erosion the crest of the mass was carried northward so that it occupied a position now approximately represented by the main ridge from Whitley's Cove to the west end. Following this came the irruption of the porphyrite laccolite, possibly preceded by a further tilting of the block. This irruption led to the formation of a structural valley in the Little Harbor region, between the porphyrite area and the ridge just mentioned. This valley was subsequently enlarged and deepened by an extensive erosion which followed. At this time Catalina probably stood some two or three thousand feet higher than now. The mass then had the general form of two long ridges, the one already referred to, and another having the general trend of the porphyrite area as seen on the map, and being possibly connected with the former ridge not far from its eastern end. The drainage of the large valley just mentioned was to the west. Its remnants still exist on the island, forming the amphitheater of the Little Harbor region.

This period of erosion was followed by the eruption at intervals of andesite, which completely filled a portion of this valley and covered the adjacent ridges. The source of these outpours appears to have been local. They were accompanied by a slow settling of the land area to which this mass then belonged, and Santa Catalina became an island, probably for the first time in its history. The evidence shows that it has remained an island ever since. That it was sinking at this time is shown by the deposits of tuff intercalated with the lavas.

This submergence continued after the andesite flows had ceased, for the higher portions of the andesite were somewhat eroded before the island had reached its lowest level, as is shown by the fact that the shelly deposit near Orizaba (see page 51) lies in a saddle several hundred feet below the peaks bordering it on either side. The amount of this depression was between 1,400 and 1,600 feet below the level at which the island now stands. That it was at least as great as this is shown by this same shelly deposit, which occurs at an elevation of about 1,360 feet; and that it was not greater is shown by the base-levelled summits of the island at an elevation of from 1,400 to 1,600 feet. This took place during Miocene times, as the deposits of shale near the isthmus bear witness. This submergence may have been sufficient to form two islands of the mass, the channel between them extending from a little to the west of the isthmus, three or four miles to the east. This is based on the fact that between these points the main ridge falls considerably below the 1,400 ft. level. It may be, however, that this decrease in altitude is a part of the local depression hereafter suggested in connection with the isthmus.

The submergence was followed by a long period of erosion, during which the then existing island (or islands) was reduced to the peneplain condition. The main body was a low and nearly level area, above which, near the center, projected the higher andesitic peaks. This area contained a bay of considerable size, occupying the Little Harbor region. The reduction of the island to a peneplain was followed by an elevation, the amount of which is approximately indicated by the 350 feet submarine contour, thus making the altitude of the peneplain, roughly, 1,850 feet. This movement was gradual, and was interrupted by at least one pause, at an elevation of 600 or 700 feet above the present sea-level. This is shown by the levelled slopes in the lower portion of the Little Harbor region, and by the sedimentary deposits found on these slopes. The island remained at its highest level long enough to carve the broad submarine bench on the most exposed side. A very slow subsidence may have taken place at this time. It was followed by the present period of comparatively rapid sinking.

This most recent period has been a short one, as is shown by the small amount of cliff cutting, which has taken place since it began, on those parts of the island most exposed to wave action. It was during the period of rapid submergence that the stream valleys of the present drainage system were flooded in their lower portions (see Plate III, fig. 1, and fig. 1, page 4). For while the broad submarine platform was being carved about the island, whatever subsidence there may have been was not too rapid for the cliff cutting easily to keep pace with it. Thus no valley drowning could take place, and no trace of buried channels or sunken valleys (belonging to the present drainage system) is found, in general, below a depth of 250 feet.

The recent tilting of the island, which has been mentioned, appears to have occurred largely if not wholly during the island's emergence after its reduction to a peneplain. For the constancy of the depth of the more recent submarine features clearly shows that their relative attitude cannot have been appreciably altered since the time of their formation, and therefore that the tilting must have preceded this in greater part, at least. To this recent differential elevation is due, in part at least, the long, narrow channels of the southern side of the island, as contrasted with the open valleys on the north; though these are doubtless due in part, also, to the more rapid cliff cutting on the southern coast.

. The present drainage system of the island was begun at the time of the last rise, after the formation of the peneplain. This peneplain has since been deeply dissected and eroded, till only the roughly levelled summits of the ridges remain to mark its former existence. Sufficient time has elapsed since the streams began their work for the gorge of Silver Cañon to be cut down through more than 1,400 feet of rock, while in the same time the broader valley back of Avalon has been excavated and its slopes minutely carved. The topography, then, is by no means young, but it has not passed its prime. The submergence and rapid cliff recession tend to preserve the youthful appearance of the island, by shortening the stream channels, thus increasing their grade and causing the streams to continue their sharp, incisive cutting. To such a cause is due the dissection of the alluvial fan back of Avalon.

The isthmus is a particularly interesting feature of the island, for the mass is nearly separated at this point. A very slight further subsidence would be sufficient to form two islands. That the isthmus once formed a watershed, which separated the two stream valleys to the north and south, there can be no doubt. These drowned valleys now form the harbors on either side, and constitute the most pronounced example of valley drowning on the island. The drainage into them was principally from the tributary cañons. The valleys were shallow, with only a gentle grade from the divide to their mouths, so that a comparatively slight subsidence has almost completely drowned them. The divide of the isthmus was at one time somewhat lower than at present, the pass having been filled in to a certain extent by alluvial deposits from the neighboring slopes.

Although the harbors at the isthmus conform to the types of the present stream topography, we cannot suppose that the isthmus itself has been formed wholly by steam erosion during the present topographic cycle. The break in the continuity of the mass, which is found at this point, is too sudden and complete to be considered as due to the forces of erosion alone, in view of the fact that no such effect has been produced in any other portion of the island. The origin of the isthmus must be otherwise explained. The most reasonable hypothesis is that of a local sag at this point. This is borne out by the sudden change in the dip of the bed of tuff and diatomaceous earth, as it approaches Isthmus Cove (shown in Section A on the map). If this is due to a local depression, that depression must have occurred before the island had reached the highest point in its last rise, and after the deposition of the tuff and shale. The submarine platform at this point shows no apparent depression, so that any sag which there may have been must have taken place before the platform was carved.

In conclusion it must be said that the writer's work upon the island was, owing to limited time, necessarily incomplete, and many details remain for future investigation.

The writer wishes to express here his gratitude to Prof. Lawson for his kindness in giving advice and assistance throughout the work. Acknowledgements are also due to Dr. J. C. Merriam.

Geological Laboratory,
  University of California, Oct. 1st, 1896.

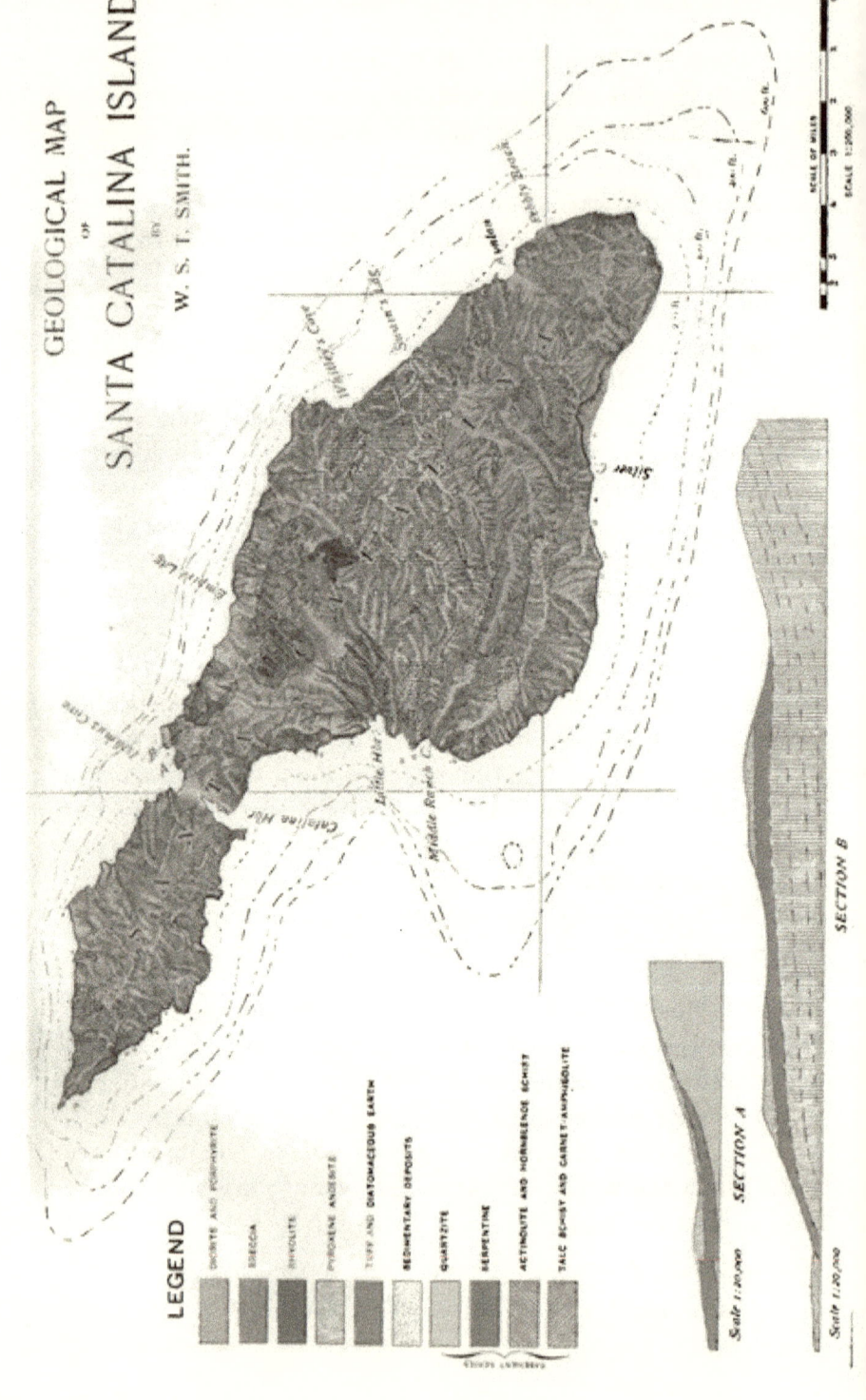

Southeastern extremity of Santa Catalina, showing breccia near the center, extending into the porphyrite on the left.

FIGURE 1—BEDDING OF BASEMENT ROCKS, CHERRY VALLEY.

FIGURE 2—AVALON HARBOR, A DROWNED VALLEY.

www.ingramcontent.com/pod-product-compliance
Lightning Source LLC
Chambersburg PA
CBHW020237090426
42735CB00010B/1734